CHASING HER

KAT T. MASEN

Kat T. Masen

Chasing Her

A Stalker Romance
The Dark Love Series Book 3

ISBN: 9798691795190

Editing by Nicki at Swish Design & Editing
Proofing by Kay at Swish Design & Editing
Cover Image Copyright 2021
First Edition 2020
All Rights Reserved

PROLOGUE

She stumbled along the path, her body grazing against mine as she chattered incessantly about the football game she just left.

I stayed on guard, knowing she wasn't capable of walking much farther in her intoxicated state. She linked her arm with mine, and it took a hell of a lot of restraint not to let the feeling of her touch cloud my judgment.

Even in the dark night, she was *beautiful*. I had been mesmerized by her since sixth grade, the way her smile made her whole face light up, showcasing her cute dimples, to her chocolate-brown locks which flowed down her back.

But she only ever saw me as the loser who lived next door.

"Julian, do you think I'm the prettiest girl in school?" She giggled, the stale stench of beer on her breath.

Of course, she knew she was the prettiest girl in school, and it being our senior year, she knew she'd be crowned homecoming queen. I had no doubt she deserved the title, I just didn't understand why she belittled herself by hanging out with the football team. They were a bunch of brainless jocks, and all they wanted was to play football, get drunk, and boast about their sexual conquests. Chelsea was one of them.

"C'mon, Chelsea, you know you are." My voice was timid. I wasn't exactly comfortable around girls, and what did I know about expressing my feelings?

She let out a laugh. "I bet you've dreamed about me and probably jerked off all over your sheets."

I felt the heat rise into my cheeks, almost certain I was blushing. Like I said, I wasn't comfortable around girls and fairly sure I might have been the only virgin in my senior class. What made it awkward was that I *had* thought of her, like every night, when I went to bed and attempted to go to sleep. I couldn't control the sexual desire I felt toward her. I had no idea what it meant, but of late, it had been almost every night.

I didn't answer her. Thankfully, we'd arrived at her house. I knew her parents were heavy sleepers, which is how she got away with sneaking out every night.

"I don't want to go home. C'mon, Julian, let's have fun," she whined.

"Chelsea, we have finals tomorrow. You need to sleep."

Without warning, she pulled my body, flush with hers. I was so close I could pick up the scent of her shampoo, *vanilla something*.

"I've got it covered. Let's take your mom's car out... maybe you could take me out to Willow's Peak?"

I stirred slightly at the thought. Willow's Peak was a notorious make-out spot. You didn't go there unless you were going to get laid, hence, why I hadn't been. I couldn't help but feel nervous. If there was any girl I should lose my virginity to, shouldn't it be with the girl I was hopelessly in love with?

We drove up to the peak which wasn't far from my house. On the ride over, Chelsea fiddled with the radio settling on The Cardigans 'Lovefool.' Belting out the lyrics, she sang loudly, tossing her hair around lost in the moment.

As I parked the car, the nerves kicked in, and a thousand thoughts ran through my head. *What the hell do I do? What if I do it wrong?*

She fumbled with her seat belt, giggling to herself as she attempted to unbuckle it. I couldn't look her way, and instead, I stared out the window into the dark sky, pretending to be fascinated by the starry night when really, I was having a panic attack. She climbed into the back seat and motioned for me to follow her.

Shit. This was it.

I followed her lead because I had no idea what to do. Why didn't I watch porn or something instead of reading back issues of *Playboy*? Breathe. I can do this. *Just don't blow your load too early.*

Climbing over my lap, she gently rubbed herself against me, my hard-on unavoidable with this pile of nerves I was feeling.

"Relax," she whispered.

She slid her hand into my boxers until her fingers were placed firmly around my dick. I yelped at the sensation. It wasn't what I expected—it was even better.

Reaching into her bra, she pulled out a condom.

God, why didn't I pay more attention in sex ed?

I don't know how she got it on as I was caught up in my own embarrassment. She shifted her body again until I felt a warm sensation spread over my shaft, and like a butterfly effect, it began to spread throughout my body reaching all the parts of me I never knew existed.

With slow motion, she began riding me, slowly grinding

until her movements picked up. The feeling was consuming me. I didn't want to tell her this was my first time, although I suspected she knew by my lack of confidence.

"Julian, I want you to remember your first time. I know how much you want me... now you have me forever engrained in your memory as the first girl who made you feel this way."

Her words echoed in my head. She'd forever be the first girl that made me feel this way, and I had no doubt in this very moment that I wanted her to be the last.

Somehow, I found my confidence and placed my hands on her face, the affection stopping her movements as I stared into her eyes. I only saw this beautiful girl, the one who had tortured me with her perfect body, the one who would throw rocks at my window to wake me up so she could ask for my English notes, not realizing how sheer her nightie was. The girl with the most enchanting honey brown eyes I had ever seen.

"Chelsea... *I love you.*"

It rolled off my tongue, and something in her eyes, the way they reflected back at me, told me I was the first to ever say those words to her.

"You l-love m-me?" she stuttered.

I nodded, moving my lips toward hers. She allowed me to kiss her, stroking my tongue with her own. It was enough for me to feel the sensation coming on like a wave of intensity and the unknown pleasure becoming part of me. The climb was greater, and with her lips pressed against mine, the feeling spread throughout me, barreling into a beautiful finish.

My breathing was uneven as I tried desperately to suck in air to control myself. *Holy shit, I just had sex!* I wanted to yell from the rooftops, a smirk permanently fixed on my face. *I just had sex with the girl I love!*

Pulling herself off, she collapsed beside me. As the windows fogged up, she opened the door, and we both climbed out for air, welcoming the cool breeze.

"You said you love me." Chelsea grinned. God, she was so gorgeous.

"I did." I smiled back, pulling her into me.

With her in my embrace, she wrapped her arms around my waist then grabbed the keys from my pocket.

"What are you doing?"

"What does it look like I'm doing?"

There was a thrill in her voice that was Chelsea, always pushing the limits. Even when we were in elementary school, she'd dare me to pull pranks on our neighbors for the fun of it. She never grasped the meaning of consequences, and her parents had always been oblivious to her wild side.

"Chelsea, c'mon, my mom will kill me. And besides, you don't have your license."

"Julian, you love me, right? So, trust me." She started the engine, the roar drumming through the isolated area surrounding us, then closed the door behind her. "Look, let me just test the car out... to the lake and back."

I could see the lake in the distance—it wasn't far. It was late at night, and no one else was around. Chelsea couldn't do anything wrong. She blew me a kiss and reversed the car, driving past me. I watched the tail lights as they drove away, the music turned up loud. I laughed, seeing the shadow of her head bopping away until, in a split second, the car hit a giant rock and spun out of control. The car tumbled over fast, and I ran, trying to stop it, but the speed outdid me and smashed against the large willow tree.

I ran for my life, my chest hurting, and the panic rising.

I screamed for help, knowing the smoke from the car was troublesome. Only a few more feet, and I could pull her out of the wreckage. A few more feet...

Until the sound of the explosion threw me back, and the flames engulfed the car.

I screamed her name into the night.

She was gone.

ONE

I gaze at the ceiling where the fan spins out of control, and my eyes flicker, unable to focus. The moans intensify, I hear them, loud, almost piercing. A slight stir awakens me. I stiffen, not wanting to fall back into the morbid place my mind is calling home.

But I am weak.

The feeling starts to build, and I hear her call my name like a purr from a wild animal, a carnivore circling its prey. I feel her stroking me, the sensations feel wrong, but they're all I have now. The control, I'm losing it.

Just one more time.

I see her face.

And I explode.

It rips through me, powerful and destructive all in one fleeting moment, forcing me to grip the headboard, my knuckles turning white, and every muscle in my body tensing from the ferocity.

I'm done.

Satisfied, she pulls away, running her tongue from the edge of her mouth along her stained lips. Her chestnut hair falls over her shoulders, and she quickly sweeps it away, exposing her naked torso. I stare because it's nice, but it's not beautiful, and it's not *her*.

I can see in her eyes that she wants more of me, a part of me I don't want to give, simply can't give. She wants my soul. She wants to own me.

"What's wrong, buttercup?" she hums as she leans over to the nightstand and pulls a cigarette out of her purse.

I hate smokers. It's a nasty habit and a serious turn-off, but one she argued as a non-negotiable if I want to fuck her.

"Don't light that in here."

"C'mon, give a girl a break. I blow ya dick that hard, I deserve a fucking medal," she gloats.

As she attempts to light the cigarette, I pull it out of her hands and throw it in the trash can beside my bedside table. Angrily, she huffs and folds her arms. Her tits are pushed up, the silicone looking about ready to explode from the force.

"I'm really over this, Julian. What the fuck do you want, huh? One minute you're ignoring my calls, and the next, you're begging me to fly here so you can screw my brains out."

The answer is simple—*I want Charlie*.

And Roxy isn't *her*, no matter how much I try to change her. Her hair may look the same, but it lacks the shine, the floral smell, the way it softly falls, allowing you to run your hands through it.

"I'm hopping in the shower. Please be gone when I'm done."

"Are you fucking out of your mind?" she shrieks, grabbing my arm and pulling me back to her. "First, you make me dye my hair, then you send me to Lex's place to fuck him, again. It's not my fault that backfired in your face! Does she fucking wear the same perfume and clothes you buy for me? I'm not a fucking fool, Julian. I look exactly like her. I'm just waiting for the moment when you scream her name during sex and not mine."

It almost happened, or should I say I've had to bite my tongue every time.

"Roxy. Leave. Now."

"Gladly. Don't go fucking calling me again to fulfill your sick and twisted fantasies."

Roxy grabs her clothes and quickly puts them on. Fully dressed, she heads for the door but stops to face me. "I'd watch my back if I were you. If Lex Edwards gets wind of this, you're dead fucking meat. I wouldn't mess with him anymore... or his wife." Roxy slams the door behind her, leaving me to bask in my own pity.

She's right. I have been lucky not to be caught out by him.

I was playing with fire, knives in hand, standing at the edge of the tallest building, and with one gust of wind, *dead*. If Lex knew what I've done, what I do, you might as well pay your respects now.

But I'm not that stupid.

And I'm always one step ahead of him.

Bowing my head, I sit at the edge of the bed, trying once again to figure out where I went wrong and how the fuck I let myself get to where I am now.

Charlie is the one, the only woman who makes me forget Chelsea ever existed. I knew it the moment I laid eyes on her that day at the gym. Sure, there were similarities, uncanny similarities, but only physical ones.

She's perfect in every way, unbelievably beautiful and sexy, not to mention intelligent, witty, and knows exactly what she wants in life. And she is the most amazing fuck I've ever experienced.

I know women like her don't just fall into your lap. Most of the time, they get loose nuts in their head or are bitten by the marriage and baby bug. I've had my share of clingers, but Charlie is nothing like those women.

Everyone warned me she was too good to be true, so I proposed to her after a few short months. Why the fuck not? She satisfied every desire of mine and gave me hope of a future without the nightmares which continue to plague me since Chelsea's death.

When she said 'yes,' I couldn't have been more ecstatic. Turns out, marriage and starting a family isn't so bad if you've got the perfect woman by your side.

I wanted her—all of her—the entire package. She'd be my happily ever after, and most importantly, Chelsea's ghost no longer haunted me.

But with anything good comes the bad, and I still remember the moment she withdrew—if only I knew why.

"Gorgeous, you're tense. Bad day at work?"

Charlie's shoulders stiffened. She normally enjoyed when I massaged her. In fact, it always led to me taking her from behind, pulling on her hair and whispering profanities in her ear just the way she liked it.

"Yeah, something like that," she mumbled.

She turned around to face me, her eyes looked pained. Something was weighing heavily on her mind, but it wasn't my style to push someone if they didn't want to talk.

I moved my hand toward the back of her neck, and with a slight force, I pulled her into me. There was resistance at first until her tongue circled mine, and she moaned slightly. It

*was my cue to take what was mine, but she pulled away, out
of breath, apologizing that she needed to clear her head. She
stood up from the couch and searched for her purse, stopping
only for a moment to lean down and kiss me goodbye.*

*I clutched her arm. "Are we okay?" I asked, not that I
had anything to worry about, she was my fiancée, after all.
Charlie accepted my ring and wore it proudly on her finger.
She'd soon become Mrs. Baker.*

"Julian, we're more than okay. In fact, we're perfect."

We were perfect.

Until the day *he* walked back into Charlie's life.

Deep down, I knew there was more to Charlie than she
had let on. Yeah, okay, we all have a past. I wasn't one to
pry, and I didn't want her prying into my life, either. She
didn't need to know about Chelsea, nor the fact that the
only girl I ever loved, the girl I gave my everything to, was
burned to a crisp right before my eyes. She especially didn't
need to know that nightmares haunted me every night and
only stopped the night she first slept beside me.

I was a fucking idiot to think she loved me enough that
any ex who would stroll back into her life would be insignificant, but, of course, luck was never on my side.

It had to be Lex Edwards.

I knew who the fuck he was. I wrote an article about
him which took me months to prepare with extensive
research. I had studied his entire life. I could even tell you
his damn shoe size. He was a force to be reckoned with. His
intelligence drove him to become a mogul, and like all the
other billionaires, he led the saddest existence. Random
floozies photographed with him at all times. His dick had
been in every blonde in sight.

But even throughout all that, I had no idea Charlie and Lex had a past, and him coming back into her life would effectively end our relationship.

I tried to trust her, but when I felt myself weaken, I ran. Just like the night of the charity ball, I was weak, and so I did what I had always done when I was scared I visited my dealer. Alone, in the dark, I'd do a line as I talked to Chelsea. I told her my fears, told her I missed her, that I loved her. I prayed for a miracle that she wasn't really gone, that I was living a fucking nightmare, and I'd wake up at any moment.

Those prayers were never answered, and the nightmares were only beginning.

I wasn't stupid. I knew Charlie was betraying me. And in some sick and twisted way, I thought, let her do this, let him hurt her, and then she'll see him for what he really is. Lex Edwards isn't the man she left behind in high school, his narcissist trait will eventually be found out, and he'll break her in ways to the point beyond forgiveness.

When she said she was going to The Hamptons, I wanted to hurt her—a side of myself to this day haunts me. My dealer just got in a fresh shipment, and the timing was perfect because I had no other way of escaping. I was on the verge of doing things, dark things I allowed my imagination to conjure up, but it was almost like someone was looking out for me, holding me back from destroying everything.

I cleaned myself up enough to drive to The Hamptons, ready to fight for what was mine until I received a call from my mother dragging me back to South Carolina because Chelsea's parents took their own lives. Tortured by the death of their only child, they had driven to the same spot where Chelsea died and drove their car into the lake, drowning instantly. It was twelve years later—what would've been Chelsea's thirtieth birthday.

It rocked the community, and the nightmares started again.

I was spiraling out of control.

The days became nights, and the nights became days.

I knew I shouldn't have let Charlie go when she handed me back the ring, but I was so high on coke, I had no idea what the fuck was happening anymore.

I miss Chelsea. The pain is fucking unbearable.

The nightmares plague me, the flames visible, and my lungs hurt from screaming her name.

Life became a big blur. I lost my job in New York, and my landlord evicted me. My mother begged me to stay with her. I had officially hit rock bottom, a fatality waiting to happen.

I needed to escape my drug dealer—as long as he supplied it, I'd take it.

Moving across the country was the best decision I could've made for myself—fun in the sun, back to enjoying surfing and other outdoor sports that I used to love. California was the answer.

The universe had other ideas, or perhaps it was fate. Charlie? Living in LA? You could imagine my shock. The signs were there—we were meant to be. I just needed to make sure I didn't fuck up this time.

So here I am today, exactly eight months after the gala when I last touched her. My *gorgeous* Charlie. She was glowing in her strapless black gown, and every part of me broke down the second we touched. Her smile was enough to erase all my bad history, enough to make me believe we were meant to be together.

Enough for me to tell her I still loved her.

She told me she loved her husband, not that I believed it for a second. There were too many pauses, and I knew Charlie better than anyone else—her marriage was falling apart. Rumors had begun spreading of Lex Edwards screwing his young assistant, Montana Black. Perhaps, I shouldn't have mentioned anything to a fellow colleague who happened to work in our 'gossip' department. But nevertheless, Charlie's life was falling apart, and she needed saving.

The problem was, I allowed my insecurities to weaken my position with us, begging her to leave him for me. Every part of me prayed for a miracle, but it never came. Instead, she walked back into his arms, and I walked into another dealer's stash after three months of being clean.

I stand up from the bed and walk over to my closet. Behind my sports jackets is a slight cavity in the wall. I reach in and pull it out—the photograph of Charlie I took when we were together, naked, spread out on my bed. The lust in her eyes, the way she begged me to fuck her, I feel myself harden instantly. And with that, I reach into the cavity again and pull out the one thing I promised myself I wouldn't, the one thing I battled with myself not to do anymore, I pull out her panties, the ones I stole from her house a few months ago.

I struggle with my morals. I know it's wrong, but the obsession takes hold of me, and so I pull it toward my nose and inhale the scent.

The scent belonging to Charlie.

Like a shot of morphine, it spreads through me, igniting my senses, my greed, and my lust—all of the things I promised myself I wouldn't allow myself to feel. Tonight, I'll sneak into her place again, just to watch her one more time.

He's in London.

I'll be safe.

I can protect her.

Just one more night, then I promise to stop.

One more night.

But I'm wrong.

TWO

The loud banging on the door wakes me from my deep slumber. I turn over to look at my watch— seven o'clock.

Who the fuck?

I rub my eyes vigorously, the memory of last night flashing before me, reminding me why I'm beyond exhausted.

A faint glow filtered through the room. Her silhouette teased me, and my heart thumped so loud I was certain it would pop out of my chest. She lifted her blouse over her shoulders. Fuck, this was it. This was what I had been waiting for. Her hands reached for the bottom of her tank top, gliding it just above her stomach until she stopped. She focused on something else. Walking over to the nightstand, a smile widened across her face as she placed the cell to her ear.

An hour later, I sat still behind the bushes, irritated by the length of the conversation. No doubt she was talking to him. Fucking asshole, can't even leave her alone for an hour.

Considering he was in London for an annual conference, you would think he'd be all business.

Her movements changed, and my boredom shifted. I positioned my binoculars, hoping to continue what I had come here for. Instead, I saw the slow drop of the blinds covering my view, and she was out of sight.

Fucking hell!

I kicked the rock beside me in frustration, a stupid move as the pain ricocheted throughout me. God, you're a fucking loser, Julian. *Just like every other time I had done this, the lust was soon overcome by guilt. I was a sick bastard, and I knew the only reason I allowed myself to do it was because it replaced my addiction to cocaine.*

Surely, stalking Charlie was healthier, right?

It was my perverse way of justifying what I knew deep inside was just plain wrong.

I hear the voice from outside the hall, and it sounds vaguely familiar. I stumble to the door wearing only my boxers and a wife-beater. As I peek through the peephole, I see the face. Scrawny looking with an odd blemish here and there. I rub my eyes—no way, this can't be who I think it is.

"C'mon, Uncle Jools, open the frickin' door!"

You've got to be kidding me.

Reluctantly, I open the door to Tristan, my nephew.

"Tristan? Why and what the hell are you doing here?"

He barges in, throwing his duffle bag on the floor and placing a small bag that was draped over his shoulder gently on the coffee table. *Oh, fuck no,* duffel bags are never a good sign. They are the sign of a drifter looking for a place to stay. He can't stay with me. I'm a nomad born to wander the earth alone. I enjoy peace and quiet. I can't have a kid living here.

"Mom said you've gone off ya nut and need some company."

He makes himself at home, sitting on the couch, placing his feet on the table with his hands behind his head.

I run my fingers through my hair to calm myself down, but, of course, it doesn't work. "Tristan, you can't stay here."

"Why not? Place is big enough for both of us." He lifts a magazine from the table and cringes. I'm not wrong in thinking finance literature isn't his taste.

My place isn't huge. It's a one-bedroom apartment on top of some seedy massage place downstairs but it's all I can afford right now. I've blown so much money on coke forcing me to downgrade luxuries like a secure apartment. It isn't such a bad place, fairly modern inside but really cramped.

He'll have to sleep on the couch.

What, so now you're thinking he can stay?

"I don't have time to take care of a minor, Tristan. I'm busy enough with work and... stuff."

He will get in the way of your night activities. Find him somewhere else to stay, the sadistic voices in my head are screaming at me.

"Minor? I'm twenty-one. I'm old enough to drink, gamble, and root. I'm in California, the babes here are bangin' hot! Just outside there was this blonde... she wanted to invite me in for iced tea and shit, but I swear... and *I swear*... she was going commando. Totally wanted to fuck me." His Aussie accent isn't lost on me, although his slang is.

"Tristan, why on earth are you back in the States?" I run my hands through my hair, bothered by his sudden appearance. "Josie wouldn't just send her firstborn to her incapable brother. Remember the last time I took care of you? I almost dropped you on your head."

"I was like a year old... that was so twenty years ago."

I know my sister well enough to know she loves her son, and the thought of shipping him off would've sent her into a depressive spiral for days, not to mention Josie thinks I'm irresponsible with no future.

"Truth? Husband number four doesn't like me." There's a change in the tone of his voice. His eyes shift toward the window, my cue to change subjects and make sure I make that long-distance call to Josie to find out *what the fuck* happened. Fuck, that asshole better not have laid a finger on him.

I let out a breath, not believing I'm allowing him to stay here. Where else can he go? I have been a lousy uncle, so I guess I at least owe him this.

As I continue to look at him, I notice how much he's changed since Thanksgiving five years ago. Josie constantly emailed me pictures of Tristan when they moved to Australia because of husband number three. That ended like a bad train wreck, and so she moved onto husband number four. Tristan has grown into a man. Well, okay, maybe a man-child. He's slightly shorter than me, his physique hidden behind a baggy T-shirt with the *Green Lantern* symbol on it. His hair is scruffy and untidy, the bleached blond making him look like an Aussie surfer, and probably why he's sporting a tan as well.

"Okay, listen, you can stay here, but only for a couple of weeks, and I want to lay some ground rules." Fuck, when did I become so parental?

"Deal." He smiles.

"Number one... pick up after yourself. I don't tolerate slobs."

"Well, how do you explain your bedroom?"

"A momentary lapse of concentration that will not happen again." No, Roxy will *not* happen again.

"Right, so you screwed your brains out with a chick who gave great head, but in the daylight, her face belongs on a wanted poster?"

"Rule number two... my life is private. You want to stay here, respect my privacy."

"What are you hiding, Uncle Jools? Some weird BDSM fetish? Somewhere in here is a secret entrance to your cave?"

"Rule number three... please stop calling me 'Uncle Jools.' Fuck the respect bullshit. Yes, I'm your uncle, but Julian is acceptable."

"Okay, well now my rule, and I only have one."

"You're kidding me, kid?" I have to laugh at this one. Tristan and rules?

"Actually, two. No coke in the house. I don't want to find you OD'ing on some line you did."

What the fuck? The nerve of the kid!

"I don't do that shit anymore."

"Well, you used to, so just don't. Get some help or something."

"And two?" I ask, annoyed.

"If I stop calling you 'Uncle Jools,' you stop calling me 'kid.'" He holds out his hand to shake on it, something I reluctantly do.

"Great, now for the *pièce de résistance*." He opens the zip to his precious cargo and reveals his PlayStation 4.

Video games?

Talk about juvenile.

The last time I played was *Legend of Zelda* back in the

nineties. Right before Chelsea—don't fucking go there, *not now*.

"Listen, ki... Tristan. I'm not a video game kinda guy. Since it's your first day in Cali, how about we head down to Venice Beach?"

"Awesome, bro!"

"Yeah, awesome." I shake my head before letting out a small laugh.

The first laugh I've had in months.

We walk along the esplanade, and like always, entertainment surrounds us whichever way you turn. One can spend hours here just watching the different acts desperately trying to drum up a crowd for a little bit of cash. People of all ages glide past us on roller-skates, some on Segways. Ladies in shorts and bikini tops will casually walk by, their sun-kissed tans and long hair shimmering in the sun. Tristan stops every so often, his feeble attempt to flirt with the hoard of girls, not that effective.

"So, you're an Aussie? Do you know the Hemsworth brothers?" They giggle.

"Sure! Jason and Keith? In fact, I went to school with them."

It's cringeworthy. I don't have the heart to tell him they are referring to Liam and Chris, but feel like I need to when they walk away in a fit of laughter.

"Snobs," he yells out.

"Uh, kid... I think they were referring to Chris and Liam Hemsworth."

"Don't call me that, and who?"

"You know... the two Aussie actors."

"Oh... Thor! I knew that. Mate, the women here are hot! Damn, I've been missing out on so much in boarding school..." his voice trails off as we walk past the weights area where Arnold Schwarzenegger wannabes are showing off and trying to be the next big thing.

"How do you think I can get guns like that guy?" Tristan points to a somewhat slim guy, though his forearms are nicely cut.

"Gee, ki... Tristan, you'll need to start taking steroids or something. Have you even finished puberty?"

"Nice one... *not*! I might have to check out the local gym. You're not bad, what do you bench?"

"I don't go to the gym. I do weights at home."

The gym is where you meet beautiful ladies who have a fucked-up past with a shitload of baggage. Lesson number one—the type of women who rip your heart out of your chest, stomp on it in front of your very own eyes, then throw it back in your face saying, "Ha-ha, loser."

"Like Bruce Wayne?" he blurts out, followed by a chuckle.

"How original. I haven't heard that before."

"Really? Because you really look like—"

"Sarcasm, Tristan. Look it up."

We walk a little further past the juggling performers before stopping at a coffee cart. I order an espresso and offer to order Tristan one since the kid looks broke.

"Coffee?" He raises his brow like I just asked him if he wanted a glass of cyanide. "Mate, that's old people's drink... I'll have a milkshake."

"Milkshake? That's a child's drink," I mumble beneath my breath.

After grabbing his milkshake from another shop and my espresso, we find a bench to sit at looking out over the ocean. It's a lovely day, as beautiful as you can get in LA. I'm still not used to all the smog, not when you've visited some of the most picture-perfect beaches in the world. Still, it's a refreshing change to be outdoors.

"So, are you still a journalist?" Tristan asks.

"Yes... for the meantime."

"Why the meantime?"

"I'm looking into other things."

"Like?" He slurps on his milkshake, following it with a loud belch.

Jesus, no class.

Should I even bother going into my aspirations? He's fucking twenty-one. His resume probably consists of a string of fast-food chains. I'm not used to these types of conversations with other human beings. After moving to LA, I struggled to meet friends, especially when I was so high on coke all the time. My dealer was my only friend, or enemy, whatever the fuck you want to call him. All my friends are still in New York living the high life I left behind.

"I don't think journalism is for me anymore."

It's the honest truth, and it is something weighing heavily on my mind of late. The passion, ambition, and desire to succeed in journalism no longer ignites the spark within me. I've tried multiple times to put pen to paper. However, nothing but utter nonsense comes out. I have no idea why I told him I am thinking of changing careers. Maybe because there's a part of me hoping Tristan can gain some sort of lesson from my mistakes.

"But didn't you go to college to study that shit? Isn't it a bit too late to change your mind now?"

"Perhaps... I don't know."

"See, that's the reason why I didn't go to college back home. What's the point?"

"For academic reasons? To make sure you're educated enough to follow a career?"

"I don't need a career, I'm happy bumming it." His response is so chilled, so absolute.

Great, I have a bum on my hands. Josie obviously thought dumping him in boarding school would work wonders.

He continues to ramble on about skateboards and competitions, but I'm distracted. I know what time it is—Thursday afternoon, four o'clock, and just like clockwork, it happens... she's here.

Yes, there's a reason why I suggested we take a stroll down to Venice Beach.

Charlotte's with a woman who I often see with her, but I don't recognize her by name. She has blonde hair and a stunning figure. They're wearing their workout gear, Charlie's stomach protruding from underneath the tank top.

I remember the moment I discovered it about three months ago. Her stomach popped overnight, and there was no denying she's pregnant with her second child. I went on a bender after that, straight lines of coke every night and a mixture of pills. My dealer has practically moved in. The only thing that pulled me out of it was a warning I got from my boss telling me to get my shit together or I was gone. With my savings account drained, I have no choice but to stay clean.

To do that, I stalk Charlie even more.

It's a vicious cycle.

One I know has to stop.

I simply don't know how.

Placing my sunglasses over my eyes, I continue to stare

at Charlie making sure she can't see me. She's unbelievably gorgeous. Her hair is cut shorter, just touching her shoulders, and it's tied back in a ponytail. She and the blonde do these yoga poses, and goddammit, there's a lot of spreading going on. It's like porn with clothes on.

I'm lost in my yoga fantasy when Tristan's voice repeats, "Are you listening to me? 'Cause you seem to be preoccupied with the brunette and that hot piece of ass next to her. I would have called the brunette a hot piece of ass, but it seems politically incorrect to call a pregnant woman that for some reason."

I wince at his choice of words. "Do you always talk that way about women?"

"What way? Just pointing out the obvious." He shrugs, still eyeing them. "How about I go say hello?"

Panic sets in. "No. No, don't you dare. Plus, you need to stop hitting on women. You're cramping my suave style. Anyway, we need to go."

"Why?"

Why, Julian? Quick think of a fucking reason why.

"I'm taking you out to a Lakers game tonight."

"Mate, are you serious? Fuck yeah, that's awesome! I've always wanted to go to one."

"Yeah, awesome..."

THREE

The Lakers game turned out to be premium seats meaning the tickets cost a fortune. I have no way out of it, so I just max out my credit card and curse at myself for bringing up the idea. Sure, I had a great time, but the entire way home I'm stressing about how I'm going to pay rent next month. Journalism pays nicely, but I'm drowning in debt. Now I have Tristan living with me board-free, and another mouth to feed.

This is why you shouldn't snort lines, you fucking idiot.

As the days pass, Tristan stays out of my way. Where he goes during the day is beyond me. He talks about trying out for some acting jobs just to get some cash. I laugh at the thought of him lined up with every wannabe actor in Hollywood, but I'm made to look like an idiot when he gets a small gig in a toothpaste commercial. Well, he does have great teeth, I guess.

I dive into my work, trying to cover every story I can for the extra cash. The reality is that I need to get my book published. I've been writing a manuscript and am about halfway through it. If I can get a publisher on board, then financially, I'll be ahead, not to mention conquering the dream of becoming a published author. After pulling a few strings, I manage to get a meeting with a publisher tomorrow afternoon.

My nerves are getting the better of me, so I decide I need something to calm me down. Bring me back to reality.

Charlie reality.

I sit in my usual spot, the corner booth hidden by the coat rack. Thankfully, the menus at the café are tall, and so I hide like every other time I have done this. I glance at my watch, eleven—her usual coffee time. Without fail, she's been here every Tuesday for the past three months. She always looks flustered when she comes in, rushing with her order of a double mint hot chocolate, replacing the long black she always orders.

Last Tuesday, she was extra flustered, but fuck, she looks so gorgeous when she is. Seeing her pregnant is like a double-edged sword. I yearn to watch that glow she gives off, but the evident growth of her stomach reminds me it's *his*, and it kills me. Another man touching her—he's touching her.

"Uncle Jools!"

What the fuck?

"Earth to Uncle Jools? Mate, you okay? You look like you've seen a ghost." He grabs the menu I'm hiding behind, causing me to panic.

"What are you doing here? And don't call me that."

I nervously watch the door. Fuck! Any second now she'll be here. I yank the menu from him, pretending to be reading it, trying not to attract any attention.

"Well, you were out of juice, and I yelled for you, but you didn't hear me, so I just followed you." He dumps his skateboard on the floor, making a loud sound. I raise my finger to my mouth, motioning for him to keep the noise down, and he proceeds to give me a 'whatever' look.

"That's kinda stalkerish, don't you think?"

Talk about the pot calling the kettle black.

"Stalkerish if you're a hot chick." He leans down to look at my legs. "But clearly, you're not a hot chick."

From the corner of my eye, I search the door only to be met by Eric's stare. *Shit, Eric!*

He walks over to the counter and places an order, his back facing us. Perhaps he's forgotten who I am. Yes, surely, he won't remember me. I haven't seen him since the gala. But then again, remember it's Eric? He has a photographic memory. That time I got fitted for a tux for the charity ball, he said I was ingrained in his mind, and should I decide to switch teams, he'll be first in line with a paddle and ball gag at the ready.

He turns around and winks at the coffee guy before walking toward us.

Just breathe, it's a coincidence.

You aren't here to see Charlie.

People need coffee, I need coffee.

Yes, stick with that!

"Well, well, well... Mr. Baker. It's been a while." He smirks.

"Eric, how have you been?" I politely ask, shaking his hand.

"I've been fabulous. But you don't want to know about me, and if you do, then ding, ding, ding!" He raises his eyebrows up and down causing me to laugh. Eric hasn't changed one bit.

"I believe we've established this on more than one occasion."

"Yes, we have. But hey, men are known to swing during a midlife crisis."

"Eric, I'm thirty-three, and I have all my hair. I'd like to think it's still a while till I hit my midlife crisis."

"Okay, but if I see you driving around in a luxury sports car, I may yell, 'This guy has the smallest penis *ever.*'"

I continue laughing.

Eric has this way of turning any situation around. Here I am, paranoid that he'll know I'm waiting for Charlie. Well, at least he hasn't pointed that out *yet.*

"So, is this your kid or something?" He looks at Tristan, eyeing him up and down.

"Mate, I'm twenty-one... hardly a kid," Tristan says defensively.

"Oh, nice accent. Perhaps the skateboard threw me off," Eric replies childishly.

"Eric, this is my nephew, Tristan. He's staying with me for a few weeks."

Introductions over with, now Eric can move on his merry way like this encounter never existed.

"Nice to meet you, Tristan. So, you from the land Down Under?"

Eric's Aussie accent is terrible.

"Nope, a native southerner. Just sent to boarding school in Sydney," Tristan corrects him.

"Boarding school? Oh, how very *Harry Potter* of you. Boarding school would be like a dream come true. Stuck in a dorm room with other boys? Communal showers..." he starts to trail off as Tristan begins to look uncomfortable.

"It's kinda not like that," Tristan mumbles, his voice low.

Eric senses Tristan is uncomfortable and moves on. "So, how long are you in Cali for?"

"Officially, two weeks, but then again, it's however long Uncle Jools will have me."

I cringe again at the name and shoot him an annoyed look.

Tristan mouths the word "sorry."

"Tristan here has decided to couch surf, or should I say set up indefinitely on my couch with his PlayStation."

Eric continues to ramble on, his filter apparently deactivated. "Right, I'm not good with electronic devices. Unless, of course, it comes with—"

"I get it, Eric... your taste is somewhat controversial."

"Only to those who live a life of celibacy." Eric laughs.

I have an idea. Will it work? Who knows, but it will keep Tristan busy, which means I'll have more time to resume my normal activities. I have spent enough time with Eric to know his weakness is socializing.

"So, Eric, would you be interested in showing Tristan around? You know, all the cool spots where you kids hang out these days?"

"I don't think Tristan would, um..." he clears his throat, "... be thrilled with my hangout spots."

"Do I dare ask?"

"So, how do you feel about whips and chains?" Eric teases Tristan.

"I, um... mate, I don't..."

"Relax... it's a joke. You Aussies make plenty of jokes while you're having a shrimp on the barbie."

Shaking my head, I laugh at his cringe-worthy comment.

Tristan, on the other hand, rolls his eyes, appearing bored by Eric's antics. Well, tough luck, buddy. I need you out of my fucking hair and no better way to get you out than with Eric Kennedy.

~

I've been staring at my screen for a good three hours. My nerves are taking over—tomorrow's meeting is make-or-break time. The publisher has agreed to review my half-finished manuscript. I doubt myself, and my confidence is at its lowest. I think about pulling the plug, but this is my dream. I need to clear my mind. Nothing good will come of me sitting here and worrying about something I have absolutely no control over.

"So, I don't know what time I'll be home," Tristan pipes up.

"Okay, I'm not your dad, Tristan. Plus, you're twenty-one. Go get laid tonight. Might do you some good."

"Yeah, so Eric texted me to go hang out. Do I look okay?"

I turn to face him. He's wearing ripped jeans and a *Man of Steel* shirt. It appears he has a vast collection of DC Comic shirts.

"Eric will crucify you. But hey, he knows you're straight, so he'll probably go easy on you."

There's a cheerful knock on the door, and I open it to find a very dressed-up Eric. *Oh shit*. Tristan has disappeared to the bathroom to hopefully rectify his attire.

"Hi, Batman, is Robin here?" He chuckles.

"Very funny. Tristan is in the bathroom, he'll be out in a minute."

Eric walks in and sits on the couch, eyeing the place and scowling, though he's unaware of his facial expressions. "Quite a small apartment?"

"Yes, it is," I answer flatly.

"So, listen, before Tristan comes out, I need to tell you I told Charlie."

I quickly meet his eyes, my adrenaline spiking at the sound of her name. Fuck, just act calm. This might not be so bad.

"How is Charlie?"

"She's great. Actually, she is more than great. Look, she asked if you are okay."

She asked about me? My confidence is slowly rising, and with caution, I hold back the smile willing to spread across my entire face. Eric is intuitive, and the last thing I need is for him to interrogate me.

"Listen, Julian... she doesn't have a problem with me talking to you. But Lex, well—"

"If it's going to cause trouble..." *Act like the nice guy, Julian. You know how to put on a great act.*

"No, I can handle Lex. Just—" Tristan walks into the room and interrupts the conversation.

"Oh, dear Armani Gods. May you grant me the patience I need to fix what clearly needs to be changed." Eric shakes his head as Tristan shrugs him off.

They say goodbye and close the door behind them before Eric can finish his sentence about Lex.

As soon as they're gone, I jump on the couch.

She asked if I was okay.

That means she's thinking about me.

She cares about me.

Does she still love me?

I have to find out for myself.

Tonight, I'll go see her again.

And tonight, I will get *closer*.

FOUR

The time ticks just past midnight.

In the dark of the night, I take small steps deciding not to sit in my usual spot by the large bush. The property is surrounded by empty land overlooking a canyon with dense nature surrounding it. The area sprawls across acres of land, true to the reputation of Hidden Hills.

Despite the affluent neighborhood being a gated community, I've heard of ways to enter without being caught. Considering the information comes from my former drug dealer's circle, I don't ask how they know or why or even care for that matter.

I enter through the back fence where there's a small gap, so small the wire catches on my black shirt almost grazing my skin. I know where the cameras are positioned. The red light flickers every few seconds, and fortunately for me, they haven't hired fulltime security which gives me ample opportunity to get close enough as long as I remain focused.

Just breathe, be patient, and soon you'll see her.

I flatten my body along the fence, careful not to rustle

any bushes. Thank God that yappy dog of hers is nowhere to be seen, but I remain on guard, armed with dog treats in case it makes an appearance like last time.

On the left side of the house is a small entrance about the size of a manhole. I pull the lid off and place it gently on the ground. My hands begin to tremble, a combination of adrenaline and nerves all rolled into one. Taking a deep breath, pushing myself to continue on, I climb into the confined area then crawl through the tight cavity until I find myself in the basement.

I give myself a few moments to collect myself, scanning the area around me. There's nothing unusual, just boxes labeled and stacked neatly against the wall. Considering the house is enormous, I was expecting the basement to be cluttered, but then remember they only moved in here a year ago, and Charlie has OCD when it comes to her home.

The house itself is over thirteen thousand square feet sprawled over acres of land in Hidden Hills. I researched the property online, visiting previous listings before they purchased the house, studied everything I could to pass the time and focus on something else besides my cravings.

I also know her bedroom isn't too far from the entrance of the basement—a few feet more, and I'll see her.

I have only done this once before when they were vacationing in Mexico, so to know that she's actually here, my heart is beating a fucking million miles a minute. I swear it's on surround sound echoing throughout the house, and I'll have a heart attack.

I imagine the headlines now—*Ex-Lover Found Dead in Woman's Basement.*

Yeah, just great, that will calm your nerves.

Lost in my tragic thoughts, I somehow find myself at the entrance of her bedroom. Carefully placing my hand on the doorknob, I turn it slightly until it makes a small creak. I stop in a panic, then attempt again until the door opens, and I'm staring directly at her.

Lying on the large four-post bed, nestled between the white sheets, Charlie lays perfectly still.

My heart slows its beat, almost like it finds comfort, a form of peace it's desperately seeking. I imagine my heart decides to stroll up and sit on my shoulder, nestling itself into my neck, watching her sleep with a huge smile. Yep, we become one at this moment, losing ourselves as we watch this beauty before us sleep.

And there's no doubt Charlie's beauty is understated.

No matter how hard I try, no one else measures up to her.

The obsession runs deeper than her beauty, and at times, I even struggle to understand why she consumes me, especially after choosing *him*.

Yet, we all make mistakes, and I'm far from fucking perfect.

Does she love me? She said she would always love me.

Love doesn't just fade.

I love her.

Why else would I be so happy just watching her?

I know this much—I don't want to hurt her. I don't want to inflict any pain upon her. That's my definition of being in love.

I watch her sleep, her eyes fluttering. Her soft breathing is in perfect rhythm, her chest rising and falling. Her angelic aura forces my imagination to wander to a place of reflection of what could've been if we stayed together—we'd be married, with child, and maybe even more than one child. We would have been happy.

My posture relaxes as the thoughts calm my anxiety,

and a shallow sigh escapes my lips. But then, like a force so brutal, the tide turns. My head, content in one moment, is tensing at the realization of Charlie choosing another man, a man who I resent. One who I also find cunning and despicable, and a man who calls on people to destroy me and end my life.

Yes, I know Lex Edwards wants me gone.

That thought alone pushes my heart back into the dark hole it has been isolating in. The anger begins to swell within my chest and the room becomes suddenly stifling hot, my palms beginning to sweat as I gulp for air trying to remain as quiet as possible.

I'm having a panic attack, desperate to reach out to Charlie and force her to make all this pain go away. Her lips, they are soft, they can wash away my sins with just one kiss. The warmth of her eyes, they'll blanket me and make me feel whole again, give me the confidence I so desperately need to return to the old Julian.

And her body convulsing beneath mine, she'll make me feel like a *man* again.

In approximately one minute, I will do something I could possibly regret.

I need out. *Now.*

With light steps, I walk toward her, ignoring the voices telling me to leave. Standing beside her bed, my eyes draw toward her bedside table and the cell sitting next to a picture frame. I don't pick it up, but as if the universe knows of my wrongful behavior, the screen lights up with an incoming text.

Lex: *I love you, my wife. Always, forever, and tomorrow, I'm going to show you just how much.*

*P.S... I love it when you're pregnant, your wild
hormones ALWAYS work in my favor, baby.*

The words are like daggers, each digging deeper and
tearing apart my ego. Closing my eyes for a brief moment,
my nostrils flare like a beast ready to attack until my eyes
spring wide open catching sight of her wedding ring beside
the phone.

My fingers trace the platinum band, and next to where
it lays is a framed picture of the two of them on their
wedding day. I pick it up, recognizing this photograph when
it leaked online. Undoubtedly, Charlie looks happy, and
again, this should've been us.

I place the frame back down carefully, clenching my
teeth to contain my jealousy. Only inches away from her, I
crouch down until I make the boldest move I had ever made
in my fucking life.

I lean in and kiss her hair.

The scent shoots through me like a bullet, ricocheting
throughout my whole body. All my senses heighten, and the
fragile broken side of me knows the only way to repair the
damage is to have her in my arms.

But who?

Chelsea or Charlie?

FIVE

I sit perfectly still, my posture straight, and my eyes focused. The room is lit brightly, the fluorescent glow creating a clinical atmosphere. Trying not to appear too distracted, I shift my eyes to the pictures which grace the wall. Aligned perfectly in dark brown frames, there's achievement after achievement. Wait! Did I just see the words 'Nobel Prize Winner'?

Run, *now*.

Mr. Grimmer sits behind his large mahogany desk. His eyes are darting across the pages, allowing me to watch him. He's an older man, maybe mid-sixties. His bald patch leaves nothing to the imagination. There's a slight comb-over, but you probably wouldn't be paying attention to that because you would be too busy staring at his tortoise-shell glasses. The lenses are so thick they look like the type you would get at a gag shop. He wears a short-sleeved white shirt which has a pocket at the front, and inside sits a blue pen and a red pen. Well, shit, red could only mean one thing—an ass-kicking.

He reaches into his pocket to pull out a pen, and I watch as his fingers linger on the tip of the red pen.

Fuck! I knew it. Do I really think I can pull this off? All that cramming in Harvard, and you're going to end up in the gutter. What a waste of my fucking life.

"Mr. Baker, I have to tell you, I'm quite impressed with your manuscript." He offers a warm smile. Perhaps I'm overthinking things. He pushes his glasses back past the bridge of his nose, his face searches mine, obviously waiting for an answer.

Act confident. Don't show weakness.

"Thank you, Mr. Grimmer. I feel honored you can see my vision. As you are aware, this is my first venture into publishing my own work."

"Well, we all have to start somewhere, Mr. Baker, and you definitely have the talent to pursue this as a career. Now, what I want to see is the finished manuscript. Have that to me by September first, and if it's up to par with what I've read so far, you have yourself a publishing deal."

September first?

As in eight weeks?

How the *fuck* am I going to pull this off?

"Thank you for the opportunity, Mr. Grimmer." I stand and politely shake his hand.

With his right hand, he pats me on the back. "Mr. Baker, I have faith in you and your work. You've got something I don't see much of anymore... compassion. You can do this, son. Stay focused and keep your eyes on the prize."

I hear the loud sounds of the waves crashing on the shore as I walk along the beach attempting to clear my thoughts. Eight weeks to finish a manuscript which has taken me six months to write. The big fucking problem is that it was written when I was as high as a kite. The days when I barely slept, when I remained isolated in my apartment with the blinds closed, deep within the darkness, just my thoughts and me.

But I haven't touched that shit in such a long time.

Not since I discovered Charlie is a far better addiction.

Only, without Charlie, I have no inspiration, which leaves me with only one option—back to watching.

She'd be so fucking proud of you if she knew what you were writing, and that makes this all okay. Right? Charlie has a heart, the biggest heart I know. It's such a damn shame she wastes its efforts on scum like Edwards.

Eyes on the prize. Once this is done and published, maybe Charlie will realize what she has been missing all along—a man who genuinely loves her and only her. A man who will move heaven and earth and give her everything she deserves.

I close my eyes wanting to see Charlie's face, but the image of Chelsea's dead body flashes through my mind instead, causing my heart to temporarily stop. I clutch at my chest, pain soaring through me.

What the hell was that?

The demons are returning, the same ones that have trapped me for all these years. The same ones that linger amongst the shadows and torture me with their ghostly presence.

I need an escape now, anything to take away the pain.

The demons taunt me, their eyes thirsty for the white-laced acid.

Fucking run. Now.

I race back to my car, knowing I have to use all my strength to distract myself. The only healthy thing I can do right now is head back to my office and throw myself into work. I just need to get through today. Survive.

Distract yourself with work, I repeat in my head.

My workplace has become a home away from home. The building is located in downtown LA and is fairly new. Like any newsroom, the atmosphere is constant chaos. Employees are running around like turkeys a week before Thanksgiving, others sitting behind their partitions talking loudly on the phone. The sound of keyboards clicking at record speed echoes throughout the office, the desperate task of trying to hit that sought-after deadline.

I walk into the main foyer to be greeted by our receptionist, Nyree. She is new to our office, and I've barely had a chance to talk with her. Our phones ring off the hook, and she's constantly busy. Today, she's sitting quietly at her computer typing away.

"Good morning, Mr. Baker," she cheerfully greets.

"Nyree, call me Julian, please," I scold playfully.

"Sorry, *Julian,*" she enunciates. "I've got a ton of messages for you. You may just be the most wanted man right now."

"That depends by whom..." My eyes dance as I watch her, waiting for her flirtatious reaction to my comment.

Nyree is an incredibly beautiful woman, tall and slender with the perfect number of curves in all the right places. Her piercing blue eyes and unruly blonde hair stand out. She lets out a wide grin, handing me the messages. Our fingers touch for a moment.

Hmm, wouldn't she be a nice girl to fuck? Okay, seriously, don't mix business with pleasure, but all my dick can think about right now is pleasure. This is what happens when your nephew moves in with you, and you have no private time to jerk off. I give her a wink and head to my office, trying to hide the bulge in my pants which needs relieving.

With a mountain of work done, the day goes by fairly quickly, and before I know it, the clock reads five-thirty. The office starts to clear out when my phone rings—it's Nyree.

"Miss Parkins, staying late? Quite the productive employee," I tease.

"I have someone here to see you," she politely answers.

Fuck, I wish it was a booty call. *Seriously, Julian, go to the fucking restroom and jerk off now.*

"Sure, who is it?"

"He'd prefer to see you..."

Huh, odd. "Okay, send him in."

I tidy up my desk, making it more presentable, not knowing when she said someone would be here to see me that meant I'd find Lex fucking Edwards standing in my office only moments later.

What. The. Fuck.

I stand up and extend my hand as a polite gesture. If he sees my hand is as solid as a rock, he won't know I think about Charlie almost every second of the day, and that last night, my lips touched her. I retract my arm as it's evident he doesn't want to play along with my game.

"Lex, to what do I owe the pleasure?"

He stands at my door, his glare fierce. Lex is a tall man, pretty much on par with me. He's standing there dressed in a business suit and tie, arms folded. He's trying to intimidate me. Perhaps it's working, but all I have to do is remember that I was once inside his wife, *more than once actually,* and with that thought alone, I know I'm not the only person scorned in this room.

I motion for him to take a seat, which he declines by remaining silent.

"Do I need to be more cautious of my wife's where-abouts?" he grits.

"Excuse me?"

He pauses, trying to remain calm, but I can see the vein almost popping on his forehead. The way his words come out strained to the bitter gaze he can't seem to control in my presence.

"First, I hear that Eric is dating your nephew."

"I wouldn't call it dating, considering Tristan is straight."

"Not according to Eric," he snarls, eyes wide as he continues to fixate on me. "I can't stop Eric from doing whatever the hell he wants, but I can stop Charlotte from having any contact with *you*."

"Interesting. Your wife hasn't contacted me, and if you know Charlie, she'll do whatever the hell she wants. Remember, once upon a time she was going to marry me. I know her inside and out just like you do."

Inside and out, *especially inside.*

I watch him as his fists clench, his eyes bulging out of his head. My defense is up, and I'm certain he's going to strike at any moment. We've gone head-to-head once at the restaurant, and although I'd gladly smack my fist into his face right now, Charlie will never forgive me.

He shifts his neck, creating a slight crack. "Is there anything else you want to tell me?"

I think about his question carefully, but know I must answer promptly because my hesitation can be interpreted as guilt. He's calling my bluff, and I've studied this man enough to know this tactic will not work on me.

"Could you be more specific? C'mon, Edwards, I've got shit to do, and I don't appreciate my time being wasted."

This time, he inches closer, his hands leaning on my desk for support. "Someone has been at my house, and I'm this close to ending your fucking life right now."

I look him straight in the eye, refusing to allow Lex fucking Edwards to intimidate me despite the fact he's hot on my trail. "Do you think I'd be that stupid to break into your house? Besides, Charlie made it perfectly clear to me she's married. You won. Game over. Leave now."

"Game over?" He lets out a chilling laugh. "I believe it's still being played. I'm warning you, so listen carefully... if I catch you anywhere near Charlotte, and I mean *anywhere* near her, I'll personally hunt you down and beat the fucking shit out of you with my bare hands."

"Oh, c'mon, Edwards... if you did that, do you think Charlie would be happy?"

He almost spits out the words, "My wife doesn't get a say in this."

I laugh at the thought. I'm safe. I know Charlie. She wouldn't wish anything bad to happen to me despite my faults. But perhaps, him hurting me will effectively end their relationship, so that might be good?

"Here's the thing. Charlie loved me. Yes, *loved* me. Wanted to be with me the rest of her life... wanted kids... five, to be exact. If you hurt me, you hurt her. Simple. I'm not doing anything wrong here. I wish you guys all the best."

Lex's ragged breathing is the only noise filtering throughout the room, and I'm so close to punching his fucking face. He has Charlie, he fucking married her and made children with her. The nerve of the fucking idiot to walk in here and parade what was once fucking mine.

My calm demeanor is compromised as burning rage hisses through my body. The ferocity is like a venomous poison—the hatred toward this man engulfing my moralities and destroying my plan to climb out of this mess called my life and create a future with Charlie.

"Don't think this is over, you understand me? I'll do everything to protect my family. Watch your back, Baker." With those final words, he storms out of my office.

Sweat beads trickle down my forehead as the realization that in the blink of an eye, my life can be over. That was a close fucking call.

You fucking idiot, Julian, why can't you just get your fucking life together for once?

Now, what do I do? He's onto me like a dog sniffing the trail, but now I need Charlie more than ever. I need her to get through the rest of my manuscript.

Or I succumb to the white-laced acid.

There is no alternative.

Charlie is my only way to survive.

SIX

The night is filled with raging continual nightmares. I've tossed and turned, trapped inside my rampant imagination. I'm always just a moment's reach from pulling Chelsea's body out of the wreckage, her screams echoing through the night.

The fire blazing in front of my eyes is wild, out of control, and incinerating everything in its path.

I'm paralyzed with terror.

Chelsea!

I scream, but my voice can't be heard. My cries are silent pleas, and with force, I try, but it's as if my vocal cords don't exist.

A loud noise awakens me, my body is drenched in a cold sweat as I sit up, unable to breathe from the horror of the nightmare returning.

Burying my face into my hands, I try to erase the memories, bringing myself back to reality. With the sheets twisted around my limbs, I untangle myself willing the freedom to move around. My heart continues to beat erratically, and with exhaustion playing into the mix of emotions, I fall back onto the bed and stare at the ceiling.

Everything about me is overly complicated. The voices need to stop—the ones continually taunting me. I battle with my good angel. We have a love-hate relationship but mostly hate. It constantly whispers in my ear telling me to fucking fix my life with reminders that once upon a time I had the world at my feet.

That was until the world decided to crush me.

I must try again to get back on track. I'm not stupid, my intelligence gives me opportunities others would kill for, and then to some. I apparently have the 'entire package,' the perfect mating partner, at least, on the outside. On the inside, I'm a train wreck on fucking crack.

I'm not going to take Lex's warning lightly. If Charlie were mine, I'd do the exact same thing. Maybe that's why I battle with this decision so much. Yeah, I know he wants the best for her, but who fucking said he's best? Then again, am I? What can I possibly offer her now?

It's too much thought for four in the morning, and the only clear decision I can make is that I need to get through the next eight weeks without seeing Charlie and definitely no coke.

I start out on a roll with a fresh attitude, the writing flowing perfectly. Every night I sit in my apartment and pour my words onto the screen. It's a different type of high—a positive high. I even position my Harvard pictures near my desk, reminding me of how hard I have worked to get to this point in my life.

Life's coming together.

I *can* win this battle.

I was doing well until all hell broke loose in my head. Tristan is annoying the fuck out of me, and I need my space. Okay, to be fair, he isn't around as much. Eric's taking this tour guide thing to a whole new level. I've even seen a physical change in the kid. I had to bring it up fearing he was taking steroids.

"Listen, don't take this the wrong way, but since when did you get so big?"

"If you weren't my uncle, I'd be extremely paranoid right now." He continues to rapidly press the buttons on his control while whatever war game he's currently playing is occupying his attention.

And that's another thing—the fucking PlayStation.

I only have one television in my apartment, and forgive me for wanting to watch the news to catch up on what's happening in the world. I'm this close to throwing it out the window and claiming the apartment was burglarized.

"Just want to make sure you're not mixing with the wrong crowd." *Who the fuck am I to talk about wrong crowds?*

"I've been hanging out with some bangin' babes. If you mean wrong as in double-D hunnies, well..."

I raise my brow. "Eric hooked you up with double-D hunnies?

He pauses his game and turns to face me. "I don't always hang out with Eric. I have a life outside of him. Besides, he prefers men."

"Yes, he does. Okay, just making sure you aren't stocking up on the 'roids. Okay, kid?"

He presses play on the control. "I'm not a kid. In fact, I got a date with double-D hunny, Claudia, tonight, and considering it's at her place, I'm pretty certain you won't be cooking me breakfast."

"When have I ever cooked you breakfast?"

It's laughable. The kid eats Captain Crunch every morning.

"It's an expression. You know because I'll be busy motorboating all night—"

There's a knock on the door, interrupting Tristan's motor-boating comment. Staring into the peephole, I see Eric's perfectly styled hair looking right back at me. Oh, dear God, seriously, here comes a tidal wave of drama.

I open the door, and Eric walks right in and stands beside me. He's dressed in gym gear—the tights hugging his thin frame and other parts prompting me to look away.

"Make yourself at home, Eric," I comment sarcastically.

"Hey, Batman. Is Robin, ready to hit the gym?" He notices Tristan playing on the sofa. With a look of disgust, he turns off the television.

"Eric, what the fuck?" An annoyed Tristan glares at Eric.

"Uh, hello, *Flubber!* Gym time. I messaged you!"

Flubber! Tristan is scrawny. The irony and reference to the movie make me laugh out loud.

"No, you didn't," Tristan argues back.

Eric searches the coffee table until he locates Tristan's cell. "Here, let me prove it." He scrolls through with a confused look on his face. "Who's Claudia?"

Tristan snatches the phone but doesn't speak so I interject, "Double-D hunny who Tristan plans to motorboat tonight."

"I didn't say that!"

Eric is quiet, which is very out of character. "A date, huh? So, tell me, what do you plan to wear?"

Tristan shuffles his feet awkwardly. "Maybe that blue shirt and my jeans."

"And shoes?" Uh-oh, Tim Gunn has entered the building.

"My chucks... I think."

"Tristan, no girl wants her beaver pounded by a guy wearing chucks. Rule number one," Eric points out.

"I do plan on removing my chucks before I bang anyone," Tristan shouts, heading toward the kitchen.

"I'll argue that... I have chucks. I pound beavers," I correct him.

Eric plasters on a fake smile. "But you, my dear, are Batman. You can wear a pink tutu, and women will still want the full buffet breakfast."

Tristan walks back into the room with a bottle of water. "Buffet breakfast? As in eggs, bacon—"

Eric cuts Tristan off. "No, sweet pea, as in they want an Aussie kiss. The same as a French one but down under."

"Eric..." I burst out laughing at his pathetic analogy.

"Oh, wait! I've got a good joke I heard the other day." Eric straightens his face to tell the joke, Tristan cringing already as I suspect Eric tells him crude jokes all the time.

"How is a pussy like a grapefruit?" He waits for our response.

"How?" I indulge him.

"The best ones squirt when you eat them." He slaps his hand on his thigh and lets out a huge roar of laughter which I can't help but join in with.

"I don't get it." Tristan scratches his head.

"Go take a shower," I tell him. "Perhaps Eric can give you a lesson on it another time."

"Unfortunately, I'm more educated in that department than I should be. Rocky has an unhealthy obsession with them and isn't afraid to send me links. Once I watched a squirting contest. I swear it was like the squirting Olympics!"

I've seen the exact video, but now isn't the time to bring that up. "Give Tristan a break. It's not that easy to get laid. I think he's just trying to find his feet."

"How is it not easy? I've seen women swarm around you. In fact, it used to drive Charlie insane. Although she'd never say so since she's as stubborn as a mule." He continues to ramble on, but I'm taken back and distracted by his comment about Charlie.

Her name. Her jealousy. No, don't succumb.

There's silence in the room. *Fuck, think of something, anything!*

Eric places his hand over his mouth like a five-year-old caught saying a swear word. "Sorry, I didn't mean to bring up Charlie. I realize it might be a sore spot."

Sore spot? More like an open wound with a bullet still sitting in it. "It's fine. How is she doing, anyway?"

"I, um... do you really want to know?"

"It's fine, Eric. She's moved on... I get it."

"But have you?"

I turn to look at him, and I know he's trying to read me. I don't answer. I can't muster the courage to lie right now, so I don't say anything at all.

Eric breaks the silence. "She's doing well considering..."

"Considering what?"

What the fuck is wrong with her?

"Nothing alarming, considering she's up the duff again. Her cravings are making me gag. Last night it was bread dipped in ice cream." He does that fake dry heaving for a moment.

"Oh, well, yeah, that has to suck, right? My sister, Josie, was the same and look what she gave birth to."

There's more silence, and I'm gathering the feeling there is more to this than Eric cares to share.

"Am I missing something here, Eric?" I question.

His eyebrows perk up. "What are you talking about?"

"Charlie?"

Pursing his lips, he shakes his head. "No... that's it."

I decide to drop the conversation, not wanting him to conjure up thoughts in his head regarding my feelings toward her.

"So, what do you and Tristan do? I don't get to speak to him much despite him living here."

I'm on parental duty. Odd, I know. It isn't that I don't trust Eric, I just know there are some bad crowds in LA, and I don't want Tristan near them. My sister will crucify me.

"Been showing him all the hot spots in LA. Taking him to the gym... I don't know, just stuff us young ones do."

I ask the question directly. "Look, is he using anything to bulk up?"

Eric laughs. "Tristan? O.M.G., no, he just enjoys the weights. So do I... well, not to do them, but there's this trainer, Mitchell, and *wow*! You should see his pecs. First class. I could eat a five-course meal off them."

"Too much info, Eric."

Tristan walks out of the bathroom wearing only a towel. He's dripping wet. I notice that he has formed a six-pack. Shit, the kid is becoming a man. It isn't that which catches my attention, but the fact that Eric's mouth is gaping.

Oh shit.

This is heartbreak waiting to happen. I don't have the

heart to remind Eric that Tristan is straight, but I'm fairly certain Tristan is a big enough boy to tell him on his own.

Eric straightens up and walks over to Tristan. "Okay, show me this damn shirt."

I decide to leave them alone as I need to clear my head. Grabbing my keys, I head out of the apartment with Eric's voice on high volume. "This shirt belongs in the clearance rack at Wal-Mart! If you want a crack at this bird, you need to show off your body."

I can hear the muffled voices and decide to leave the divas to their own. I have more important things to worry about. And Eric's namedrop has become one of them.

I haven't seen her in two weeks, the urge still fighting for top position. All I have to do is make it through another night, one step at a time.

And ignore the fact that her *husband* is in Manhattan, according to the media.

She's all alone.

A temptation too hard to stay away from.

SEVEN

The one thing I love about living in California, aside from the warm weather, is that no matter where you go, you will always find something new. Sometimes it's a new eatery, a new bookstore, or maybe just a new spot to sit and ponder.

When I first arrived here, I had stumbled upon this place when I managed to get lost heading to a meeting. The meeting was being held at my boss' house—a mansion in Bel Air worth a hell of a lot of money. I remember pulling the car aside trying to google my location with barely any service, and frustrated at the time, I went to throw my damn cell into the bush when I noticed the view in front of me.

It was a farm, nestled behind a hoard of trees. There were beautiful horses grazing throughout the wide space. Their stunning manes glistened in the morning sunshine. It was picturesque, tucked away in a hidden part of the hills. I sat there mesmerized by how they interacted with each other. I'm not a huge animal lover, but for the first time in my life, I was so captivated by the beauty of the creatures that before I knew it, I had been sitting there for over an hour watching them—and was ridiculously late for my meeting.

I have been back there twice at my lowest moments, and I know the urge to visit is calling me now. I look at my watch seeing it's already after five. I've been aimlessly wandering the streets for hours without any destination in mind. It's too late to head out there now, so instead, I find myself a quiet little café.

Then, the familiar feeling of loneliness consumes me at this vulnerable moment. The feeling of being alone, of being unloved, knowing there isn't anybody out there thinking about you right now. No one to open the door when you arrive home, jump into your arms, tell you how much they've missed you.

No one to look into your eyes and feel their gaze penetrating every part of your soul.

I close my eyes. Pools of brown eyes watch me. Call me. Beg me to save them.

I miss her so much my chest aches.

Chelsea... Charlie... Chelsea... Charlie.

You fucking piece of worthless shit, you don't know what you want.

How the fuck can you fight the fire when you don't know who's igniting the flame?

The weakness. I can't be alone with my thoughts right now, so I haul ass back home. In a desperate act, I reach out to the two closest people who could possibly save me from myself right now—Tristan and Eric.

It has come to this.

Tristan and Eric aren't my saviors tonight. Tristan said Claudia isn't feeling well, and he also feels ill from something he ate at dinner, and so he isn't up for anything. Eric says he's busy, and I'm not going to ask questions. I figure it has something to do with Charlie, hence, why he's so vague. Either that or he's doing something illegal, in which case, I still refuse to ask questions.

All I know is that I need physical contact with another human being. I yearn to feel the desire from a woman, and in other words, get laid—pronto.

Alone at a bar on the corner of pathetic and worthless streets, I find myself a stool and make acquaintances with my long-lost friend, Johnny Walker.

The place is busy, people cramming themselves in. The music blares loudly but is muffled by the drunken chatter. There's a section in the corner where people dance, and the lights are dim. I search the room looking for something nice to take home. I don't give a fuck if Tristan's home, my dick has its own agenda and needs a fucking release.

As I watch the dance floor, the music changes, and the dancing slows. A woman wearing the tightest hot pink dress is playfully staring at me, licking her lips and pretending to suck the tip of her bottle. Okay, so I'm fairly certain she's all show but gives poor head. Beggars can't be choosers, I guess. I'm about to walk toward her when her boyfriend grabs her arm and pulls her in a different direction.

Damn, back to square one.

After my fifth scotch, the music makes me happy. Everyone looks like they could be my best friend, including the blonde who eye-fucked me from the dance floor. I make my way over to her and immerse myself in the tight crowd. I'm not shy—let's get this shit over and done with. I place my hand on her hip and pull her into me. She makes a slight squeal but laughs it off as she runs her hands along my chest.

I lean down to her ear to inhale her cheap perfume. *Who cares that it's cheap? Just get fucking laid already.*

"I need your name if you want me to scream it out while I'm fucking this pretty little ass of yours."

She lets out a sigh and rubs herself against my throbbing cock.

Green light.

"My name is Tori, and I need your name if you want me to moan it while I'm sucking on your cock."

I press my body against hers. I can smell the moisture between her legs. She's fucking wet as hell.

My tongue is just shy of her ear. "Julian, and we should get out of here, *now.*"

Tori continues to rub herself against my cock, my jeans constraining the poor fella as he can barely breathe, suffocating behind all the fabric. Why is she delaying?

"I'll tell you what, Julian... how 'bout we have some fun?"

Oh great.

The last time a woman said this to me, she wanted to fuck while we took Ecstasy. Sure, the sex was off the fucking charts, but I'm trying to stay clean. I think it's time to pull the plug on Tori.

"Don't look so frightened, handsome." She turns me and wraps her hands around my waist. "You see that blonde by the bar? The one with the short white dress?"

Big fucking tits—yes, of course, I see her.

"Well, how about she joins us? You know, make this more... let's say... dirty."

Jackpot.

She pulls my hand toward the exit and nods to the other girl to follow us. Outside the bar, I push Tori against the wall, crushing my lips on hers. Yeah, I am fucking desperate.

Her taste is sweet like passion fruit flavor or something.

Who the fuck knows? My dick is leading the charge here. She pulls away only briefly to hold my hand and lead me around the corner to a hotel. We enter the lobby and wait for the elevator. Once inside, I push her against the wall, this time sliding my hands up her dress to cup her ass. She moans into my mouth, but we're briefly interrupted when the doors ping open. We stumble to her room. Inside, there's no waiting. She unbuttons my shirt and runs her hands down my chest, carefully moving them along my abs.

My belt buckle echoes through the room as the metal hits the floor along with my jeans. Tori positions herself on her knees, caressing my cock through my boxers. Goddamn, the pre-cum is oozing out. *Fucking suck it already.*

I flinch as she pulls them down, and I'm bare, waiting, ready, needing her lips to wrap around it, wanting to feel my tip touch the back of her throat, wanting her muscles to choke as she takes me all in. This delayed gratification bull-shit is normally hot, but I need a release and I need it now.

Her tongue gracefully circles the head of my cock, spreading myself all over her lips. I place my hand on her head and wrap her ponytail around my hand, forcefully pulling her in. I jerk as I feel her throat enclose on my cock, causing her to gag. I let out a moan and repeat the action until I hear the click of the door.

I close my eyes and wait for her touch. *What was her name again?* Jesus, who gives a fuck.

The warmth of her body presses against my back, her nipples erect as I feel them protrude through her dress and against my skin. She runs her hands along my torso from behind, making her way down to Tori's face where she places her hands on her cheeks gently before directing her head to take me in deeper.

My body reacts instantly. The familiar pressure is

rising. *Self-control, Julian. C'mon, you've done this a thousand times with women hotter than this.*

Don't. Fucking. Go. There.

Okay, clear train of thought.

There are two women here, so let's have some fun because God knows I deserve it.

Big tits moves toward my front until her face is in line with mine. I crash my lips onto hers, her kisses frenzied, and her moans loud. She's begging me to suck on these beautiful tits of hers. I don't break the kiss. My fingers trail her body until they're dancing around her bra. With one swift move, my hands are tweaking her nipples, squeezing her tits, barely able to caress them in my hands.

They are fucking huge.

I lean my head down, ripping the dress, exposing her tits. My tongue rolls around her erect nipples, tugging them as she demands I bite them harder. I continue doing so until a warm breath engulfs me, and Tori is by my side taking her in as well. I tilt my head to the left, shoving my tongue into Tori's mouth, wanting to taste it all.

Her eyes lock onto mine, and that desire, the raw sexual appetite, consumes us in that one gaze.

She wants to taste her wet arousal.

And I want to taste her as well.

Like hungry lions fighting for their prey, we both take her to the bed and lay her spread wide, ready to devour every inch.

And just like in the wild, I take her first, tasting every part of her. Pushing her to command I fuck her instantly, but I don't. I stop and back away.

Tori makes her move, and I witness what I came for.

The scene is paralyzing any rational thoughts I have. My mind is clouded, my body is reacting in a way I haven't felt in a long time. The volcano of pressure is building from within, and I tense, trying to divert the spasms threatening to consume me. Instead, I close my eyes and take a few deep breaths.

Upon opening my eyes, I have control again.

But watching Tori gliding her tongue along her clit is enough to bring back the feeling.

In the blink of an eye, I'm protected and ready to take this one home.

I slam into her with force, her yelp is more of a cry as I push down deeper. Her walls are caving, and I feel the sensation surround my throbbing cock. I pull out, her desperate pleas begging me to enter her.

But I don't.

Instead, I tell her to lie the fuck down because this time, it's her turn to be the prey.

And goddammit, I'm going to hunt her down until every single fantasy of mine is satisfied.

We have all night.

And these two ladies are ready to *play*.

EIGHT

"I have two words for you. Beach. Party," Eric announces.

Here we go.

It's way too early for this shit. I have a sex hangover, the best kind which leaves you so fucking sore in parts you never knew existed. Perhaps, I'm missing the whole point of being single. Who needs relationships when I can have two girls suck my dick at one time?

Two girls who ate each other out like it was a marathon.

Two girls with no objections to me fucking them in their pussies *and* their asses.

One girl who had no issue with me fucking her tits until I came all over her face, only to watch Tori clean it all up.

That was un-fucking-believable.

"Ahem... I feel like I'm the giant gay in the room being ignored," Eric pouts.

Tristan scratches his head. "Eric, I think you mean elephant."

"Are you calling me fat?"

A yawn escapes my mouth. "Can both of you just shut up, please, for just a second? Actually, make it an hour."

So, this is the thing, the PlayStation isn't as bad as I first thought. In fact, it's a welcome distraction.

I've been on a high, a clean high, since last night. I blew my load twice, the much-needed relief I was after. On top of that, I'm making positive progress on my manuscript. Tristan even commented that I was in better spirits, and after a few beers, it led to him showing me how to play this game. Sure, I suck. Tristan said we make a great team, and so five hours later, we're deep in the middle of a mission when Eric comes over.

Concentrating on the screen, Tristan yells at me to watch out on my left. My palms are sweating, my ammunition low until the screen goes black. *Huh?*

My head spins quickly to look at Eric. "Eric! It took us hours to unlock that path."

Eric's face falls. "Look at yourself, Batman. You should be outside with the rest of the world parading what you got, not holed up in here playing games. Think about the number of women lying in their lonely beds right now wishing a hot man like yourself will save them from their rabbit and personal hell."

"Hey! What about me?" Tristan argues.

"I've still got a beef with you after you dodged our last gym session, and I walked past you at the Dairy Queen stuffing your face."

"Yeah, well, I was hungry."

"A minute on the lips, forever on the hips. Anyway, get your asses changed. There's a happening beach party in Malibu tonight, and I, for one, need some wiggity wang."

This is a battle not worth fighting, so I stand and head to

my room as Tristan pulls me aside. "What the hell is wiggity wang?"

I shrug. "I don't know. Eric has his own language."

Eric shouts out, "It's called wanguage, *get it?*"

The drive up to Malibu could possibly have been the longest drive that ever existed only because Eric and Tristan keep arguing over the song choice.

"What do you mean you don't listen to Jonas Brothers?" Eric asks in horror.

"Eric, as if I'd listen to boy bands. I'm more of a Metallica, Guns N' Roses kind of guy."

"Who the hell is a Metallica?"

"Did you just ask me who Metallica is?" Tristan raises his voice in shock.

I grip the steering wheel in frustration. "Oh my God, both your tastes in music are piss poor. Well, maybe not you, Tristan, so let me rephrase that. Eric, your taste in music is piss poor. I'll not play that in my car and..." I place my hand in the air as I anticipate his rebuttal, "... I don't want statistics on how many records they have sold, who's still in the closet, or who you would take to bed. Now, I'll put on Maroon 5, and let's all not talk to each other for the rest of the drive, okay?"

Like a brooding teenage boy, he mumbles to himself before pulling out his cell and placing his headphones on.

California in the summertime is just one big party. It isn't hard to miss it—the restaurant with an open bar area overlooking the ocean is lit up with a string of colorful lanterns, the music blasting over the huge subwoofers, and everywhere you turn, a nice pair of fake tits are staring you in the face. I'm not a fake-tits kind of guy I'm more of an ass man, but big breasts can be an added bonus.

Stop thinking about ass and tits for one second. Beach shorts aren't made for boners. End of story.

We make our way over to a spare table and order a round of drinks. Sitting around drinking, I spend my time deciding which lucky one I'm willing to take home tonight until Eric yells out in a British accent, *"Darling!"*

As I turn to look his way, I notice a familiar blonde wave to Eric and start walking our way. Eric stands, and they air-kiss each other on both cheeks.

"Tristan, Julian, this is Kate." He raises his eyebrows toward me. Kate looks over, and her face responds know-ingly. It hits me like a ton of bricks, she's the blonde I've seen often with Charlie at the beach doing yoga. On closer inspection, she is stunning. Would that constitute to shitting on your own doorstep?

She's wearing a coral-colored bikini top layered with a white crocheted tank. Her shorts are denim with pockets hanging below the hemline. They are *very* short, but she has the longest lean legs and pulls it off nicely. Her hair is tied up in a scruffy bun, yet something about her is easy on the eyes.

Shit! Tristan won't remember, will he?

No, he can't even remember the name of the President, except the President isn't a hot leggy blonde with an ass begging to be fucked.

My heart picks up a pace as the panic overcomes me. *Should I pull him aside to explain?* No, just play it cool, he won't remember her.

"Pleased to meet both of you, finally." She pulls up a chair and sits beside Tristan. "So, I hear Eric has been showing you around? Oh, my days, did he do his tour of the celebrity homes yet?"

"Yes, although I don't know half the people he talks about. Who the hell is Shirley MacLaine?"

Kate lets out a loud laugh. "Aren't you a young lad! Perhaps a tour of Joe Jonas' house is more up your alley."

I interject, "Please don't bring up the Jonas Brothers. The car ride over here was painful enough."

She tilts her head to the side, raising her brow while gazing at me. There's something in her stare, something warning me her beauty may only be on the outside and not on the inside. I need to remain guarded. Whatever her tie to Charlie it may quite possibly involve *Lex*.

Eric senses the shift in mood and grabs Tristan to introduce him to another friend at the bar, leaving me alone with Kate. There's an awkward silence. I'm fairly certain Charlie has filled her in as to who I am or, no doubt, Eric will have gladly done so.

"So, Julian. Keeping yourself busy in LA?"

"Work always keeps me busy, Kate."

She quiets, but something tells me the conversation is far from over. I start to put two and two together. Her British accent, she must be a friend of Lex's.

"I'm going to cut to the chase here, got no time for pussy-footing. Lex and Charlie are my family. I know Lex came to see you, and I know why." She takes a deep breath, then continues, "I get it, you were shafted, and revenge is usually the only way to redeem yourself, but think long and hard about what you're doing. They are a family, they have children. Think about how you're hurting Charlie."

"I don't know what Edwards told you, but I've done nothing wrong. I wish them nothing but the best."

"Oh, codswallop," she huffs with a confrontational

stance. "Don't think I'm another dumb blonde with no brains. Lex is like a brother to me, he's my family, and if he thinks his family is in danger, I'll stand by him one hundred percent to protect them."

For once, I know I'm not doing anything wrong. Well, I'm no longer doing anything wrong. In fact, I never wanted to harm Charlie, I only wanted to love her and have her love me in return. So, don't be afraid of this nosy bitch. What can she possibly do?

Eric's loud voice is moving closer toward us. She leans in quickly. "Do us all a favor and stay away from Eric."

Kate announces she's leaving and kisses Eric goodbye.

What the hell was that? Another person pointing out just how pathetic you are. I don't need this, and her mild threat leaves me in the foulest mood. So much for trying to let loose and have fun.

Eric senses my demeanor has changed. His voice softens as he speaks, "Was Kate being a bitch to you? Seriously, ignore her. She gets her British panties all in a twist. She and Lex just have ties that go way back."

"Are they related?" I question.

"No. She was his assistant for years, but now she runs Lexed in New York. She and Charlie are BFFs. Plus, she's Amelia's godmother... well, one of them. Kate is like the British friend everyone wishes they had."

"I see."

What do I know about friends? I lost all mine in my coke-can-be-my-best-friend stage.

"Anyway, ignore her, Julian. I know you wouldn't hurt Charlie. They're just being overprotective. You know Lex... he's obsessed with his wife."

Yes, I know, we have a lot in common. We both want to protect Charlie, but who is the enemy here?

Eric changes subjects, which I'm extremely grateful for, and starts talking about his family. I learn his father is none other than Marco Greg Kennedy, a very wealthy political figure in the business world. He has many ties with the Chinese government, which apparently is how he met Eric's mother. Before I know it, we are speaking for a while about Chinese laws, something I had no clue Eric is so educated in.

"Oh, dear God, they are playing 'Tequila'! C'mon, let's dance."

I nod for him to go ahead, and I'll catch up with him later. Tristan's already dancing with a group of girls who appear more like his crowd. His dancing, though, that's another cringe-worthy moment. *Shit, did he just do the robot?* My coconut needs refilling, and what a perfect opportunity to hit up the bar.

I get to chatting with a few girls who are hanging off me as I take a seat at the bar, numbers are shoved into my pocket, whispers in my ear, but I'm not in the mood. In fact, I can feel a familiar funk coming on. More alcohol is needed.

With everything becoming more relaxed as the liquor runs through my veins, I have no clue how I'll be able to drive home. This coconut is livening up the party, or perhaps it's the Pina Colada it was filled with. I find myself bopping to the tunes and somewhere around the song 'Love Shack,' I lose my shirt.

I'm this close to joining the conga line forming—Eric is the head of the pack.

Suddenly, heavy arms pat my shoulder. *Oh crap, I know I shouldn't have taken my shirt off.*

"Julian, dude, what's been happening?"

I turn to see the familiar face, Charlie's friend, Rocky.

Gee, looks like all her friends are here tonight. Is this a vendetta against me? You know, let's kick him while he's down? I don't feel like another lecture about being a naughty boy, so I plan to use an I-don't-feel-well excuse if needed. Sunstroke? Yes, I'll use that, except it's night, and your brain is intoxicated, moron.

Rocky plonks himself on the stool beside me and motions for the bartender to serve us. He orders some fancy beverage which also sits in a coconut, makes a comment about coconut jugs, and then carries on rambling. He sure is a talker, and I mean nonstop he goes on and on about who knows what.

I have to be polite, right? I am not the jerk everyone has me pegged out to be. "So, how are you and the family doing?"

His shoulders slump, followed by a loud sigh. Oh, why the fuck did I have to ask that question? I eye the bartender —more fucking drinks, please! This talker is going to hold me hostage, and I'm no Dr. Phil.

"Okay, I guess. Nikki didn't come tonight. We had an argument again. The whole point of coming to LA was to visit Charlie and to have a break for two weeks. But in *typical* Nikki fashion, she's in denial of everything going on, and all we do is fight. Not even hot fighting followed with dirty sex," he sulks.

"I'm sure it will work out. You've been married for a while. There's always going to be bumps in the road." There, simple and no more inviting questions.

Coconut man, where art thou!

"Bumps? *Ha!* More like mountains with a big pile of shit on top. It's not like it's all my fault, you know. It's both of us. Instead of doing something about it, she's decided to bury her head in the sand."

"Okay, you're kinda losing me here?"

Seriously, I need drinks ASAP, and the damn bartender is trying to pick up some cougar flashing her fake tits. I bang my fist on the bar, he turns around, and I believe I have caught his attention until he sways back around to talk to the cougar.

Rocky is still rambling on, unaware of my little outburst. "We've been trying to have a baby for a while now. It's not happening. I want to see someone about it. Nikki thinks we don't need to because we already have a son, so it's bound to happen again. That was like ten years ago. Things change, bodies change. I joined this trying-for-a-baby group online, and I tell you, so many couples suffer from secondary infertility. It's more common than you think."

"I read an article about it once. It affects like one in five American couples," I inform him.

"*Yes!* So, you know, right?"

Friday night at a beach party with sexy ladies in bikinis all around me, and I'm talking to a guy about secondary infertility. Life fucking blows right now. *Why hasn't that conga line come to save me yet?*

I strain my eyes, trying to focus. "Just give her time to come around to the idea. Maybe you do need medical intervention."

He chuckles loudly. "Have you met my wife? She's as stubborn as two mules. Look, I'll be honest with you, dude. It's gotten to the point that she wants to fuck all the time, and for the first time in my life, it's not fun. I know she wants to do it just to have a baby, but I never thought I'd say this to anyone... *I feel used* like she only wants me for my body."

Okay, so I want to spit out my drink and burst out

laughing. This is Rocky, after all. However, his crestfallen look tells me it's far more serious and not a joking matter.

"Rocky. You'll get through this. You need to communicate with each other. The families who were interviewed in that article said it tore their marriages apart. I can only imagine the stress it can add when, in theory, trying for a baby is supposed to be your happiest time. You're both young, and I'm sure if you take a breather, it'll work out."

Who the fuck am I right now? From stalker to counselor?

Where are my drinks?

Rocky lets out a huge belch, and some ladies near us yell "Gross" and walk away. God, this isn't helping me score at all. I'm going home alone. Alone and drunk as a skunk.

"See how pathetic I am? I'm here on a Friday night. The chick with the huge rack bounced her coconuts past me, and did I even salute her Rocky-style?" He shakes his head, disappointed in himself.

"Maybe you should head home, you know, be with your wife."

How much I envy what he has.

"I would, but she and Charlie went out somewhere to watch a show or something."

And there's that name again.

Rocky must have noticed my body language. "Oh, dude, sorry."

"Sorry for what?" I play it off.

"For bringing up Charlie. Don't know if I should have. You're probably over her, right? I mean you must be screwing babes like there's no tomorrow."

I smirk while raising the coconut to my lips and finish the drink in one sitting.

"I know that look. Tell me! I need to live vicariously

through someone else. Lex is boring as hell when it comes to talking about his past. Eric, well... forget that. I don't need a re-enactment of sucking dick."

Ahh, the blissful memories of last night. "Not much to tell. Last night was the first time in a while. They were sexy—"

"*They?*" He cuts me off, eyes practically bulging out of their sockets.

I don't respond. Instead, I remain quiet. I'm not one to talk openly about my sex life despite how nasty it was last night.

"Dude, fuck, did they eat each other out? Fuck, no, wait, did they finger each other's asses?"

I almost spit out my drink because they did, I just didn't think he'd ask.

"Let's just say, whatever your imagination thinks, it was done."

Fuck, I'm a cocky motherfucker when I'm wasted.

He lets out the loudest, "Fuck," I have ever heard and then mentions something about needing to find his wife or a bathroom pronto. Either one, he vanishes, and I'm left alone once again.

It's not for long, though.

The conga line finds me, Eric front of the train, and the night becomes one massive blur after that.

NINE

"What the hell is this?"

I stare at the drink Tristan hands me. The color is dark green, the texture thick with something floating near the brim. I feel the bile rise in my throat, and I struggle to swallow, wrestling with the vomit which is fast bubbling to the surface. I push the glass away, but his strength overpowers me. I'm weak.

Fucking Eric and that fucking conga line!

He pushes it back my way. "Drink it. I promise you won't have a hangover if you drink this."

I'm short-fused, my head is pounding like a jackhammer, and I want nothing more than to feel the coolness of the bathroom tiles caress my face. Oh, and pour that rancid-looking drink all over Tristan's head.

"Kid, fuck off. I'm not drinking that."

He continues to stand over me and doesn't let up. *For fuckin' fuck's sakes.* I grab the stupid drink off him and down it in one go.

Oh, mother of fucking.

I run for the bathroom, certain the contents of my stomach will soon be saying hi-de-ho to the toilet bowl. I wait, but as minutes pass, the feeling subsides, the headache eases.

"What the hell was in that?"

"It's best you don't know. You feel better, though, don't you?" He appears pleased with himself.

I nod, then motion for him to get the fuck out of the bathroom, and take the longest shower in the history of mankind.

The magical drink gets me out of bed and in the mood to write. Tristan goes out with Claudia, leaving me with the peace and quiet I so desperately need to finish my manuscript. Mr. Grimmer sent me an email wanting to see an update, so I was hauling major ass trying to get it done. I'd had tighter deadlines than this before, to the point where I didn't eat or sleep for seventy-two hours straight in the middle of a third-world country, just so I could get a small section printed in the newspaper. It's all part of the journalism game.

But this isn't the journalism game.

This is my heart and soul turned into words and poured into this manuscript. It's a dream, my ambition, my future all riding on this publishing deal.

Come Monday, I'm a ball of nerves again.

Sitting in my office, I'm finishing off a piece I'm doing for the newspaper when Nyree calls.

I switch on my sultry voice. "Good morning, Nyree."

"Hi, Mr... I mean Julian. I have a call for you on line two. A Mr. Grimmer." Her voice is sweet, and I know I shouldn't go there. So I don't, for now.

Picking up line two, I take a deep breath and prepare myself for the worst.

"Mr. Baker, I hope I'm not interrupting anything important?" he politely asks.

"Not at all, Mr. Grimmer. I trust you received my email?"

There's a pause. I know it—who am I fucking kidding?

"I'll be frank. The quality of your work is mediocre. It lacks that certain element, that magic."

I rub my face with my free hand. It fucking lacked being on coke. Is that what I need to follow my dream? A sweet line to seal the deal?

"Listen, son. We often find a muse. Whatever it may be, there's something, someone accompanying you on this journey. Find it again, and the writing will flow. You understand what I'm saying?"

I nod, remembering he can't see me. "I understand."

He asks to see an update in two weeks.

Until then, I have no choice.

No choice whatsoever.

The road is dark and windy, even the moon seems obscured behind the night clouds. Like every other time I've gone up this road, I do so cautiously—eyes focused, mind fractured with emotions.

This time the emotion is guilt.

I grip the steering wheel wanting so desperately to close my eyes for a moment, but my focus needs to remain on the road.

I hear his words echo in my head.

The voice telling me to leave her alone.

The threat to end my life should I dare go near her.

I want to conquer this battle. All I have to do is turn around and head back home.

Home, not to my dealer.

Weak. Pathetic. Worthless. The words scream at me.

I'm a coward.

I slam my foot on the brake, forcing the car to a halt. I sit still, heart pumping as the engine continues to tick over. It's a desperate bid to save myself from the misery and disgrace which has once again come over me.

With my last attempt to redeem myself, I slam my foot on the gas, turn the car around and head in the opposite direction.

I did it. I won the battle *this time.*

As I take a sharp turn around the bend, I notice the skid marks on the road followed by the smell of burned rubber in the air. My eyes dart to a faint light flickering by the tree down the hill. There are no other houses on this stretch of the road, and something tells me someone is down there. I pull the car off to the side of the road, grabbing my cell before quickly hopping out and running down the hill toward the light. In the darkness, I stumble on sticks and stones and hear the sounds of animals lurking around me. Fuck, it scares the living daylights out of me until my heart stops in a panic, my legs beginning to shake, and my throat runs dry.

My brain scrambles to make sense of what I see in front of me.

The license plate.

Charlie!

TEN

The adrenaline is pumping through my veins as the cries for help draw nearer.

I run so fast my chest is burning while I'm out of breath. With time not on my side, I quickly examine the car and see the door is wedged in. There's no chance I can pull it open, the magnitude of this accident crippling me with fear.

The window is slightly ajar, and I see her head resting against the shattered glass.

"Help me... help me, please." Her voice is weak, barely recognizable.

"Charlie? Charlie? It's me, Julian!" I crouch down to her level, close enough to see the blood trickling down her forehead. I try my hardest to disguise the look of terror on my face, not wanting to frighten her

"Julian?" she whimpers.

I scramble to the back of the SUV and climb in until I'm sitting beside her in the passenger seat. Without even thinking, I grab her hand to feel her pulse, trying to remember my first-aid training. Placing the pad of my two fingers on her wrist, I press lightly and begin counting the beats per minute. Doing my mental calculations, I try to determine the strength in her heartbeat.

Her pulse is faint.

First rule—remain calm.

How?

How can I remain fucking calm when the woman I love, the woman who's supposed to be my future is lying in this wreckage, her pulse barely detectable, on the brink of possibly dying in my arms? Not to mention, she's heavily pregnant with a child.

Fuck! The baby.

I pull out my cell. It has one bar of reception. With shaky hands, I dial 9-1-1.

"9-1-1, what's your emergency?"

"I need an ambulance. I found a woman crashed into a tree." The panic is evident in my voice. I reach out to hold Charlie's hand. Her eyes are wide, and they look back at me in horror. She squeezes her eyes tight, letting out a startling scream. Her lips are quivering, and she mentions the word 'baby.' Immediately, I look to her legs and see blood stains along her thighs. Adrenaline floods my system, pumping on full throttle desperately trying to escape my body.

The phone starts to crackle. "Sir? Sir? Can you hear me?" The cell beeps, ending the call.

"Shit! Charlie, where's your cell?"

"The battery died... Julian. My baby... it's coming now."

Charlie can't lose this baby. She doesn't deserve this.

Remain calm, keep her talking. Anything until help arrives, but get her the fuck out of this car, or we're both dead.

"Okay, just breathe. Charlie, I need to move you out of the car, okay? Can you move all your body parts?"

She winces, and after a few moments, she nods.

I explain to her what I'm about to do. I have to move her delicately as I'm not sure if anything is broken. *God, what if it is?* Don't. Just don't right now.

It's difficult to maneuver her body, but somehow, I manage to scoop her in my arms enough to move her out of the wreckage. I can feel the muscles in my back strain as I carry her out and walk as far away from the car as possible. The smell of gas saunters in the air. It's a ticking time bomb ready to go off.

Just like Chelsea.

Only this time, Charlie is out.

Half the battle is won.

Farther up the hill, I place her down beside the tree on a small clearing. She takes deep breaths, visibly in pain. I reach for my cell again, but as I attempt to dial 9-1-1 for the second time, the screen goes blank. The enormity and realization of this situation paralyze me for a moment. Who's going to save us now? I look back at Charlie. There's no question, pray to the Lord she'll be saved. Do what you can do to keep her alive. I have no medical training, but I have to keep her conscious. It's a waiting game for someone to rescue us knowing I won't be able to carry her up the steep hill in the dark without assistance.

"Charlie, slow breaths. Can you tell me what happened?"

She nods again as she tries to control her breathing. "I just dropped Amelia off at Lex's parents' house, and as I was driving, I felt a sharp pain in my stomach and I lost control. The baby is coming... help me, please... I don't want my baby to die." Tears cover her face. She gulps for air as the panic sets in again.

"Charlie, you won't lose the baby. How many weeks are you?"

"Only thirty-six..."

I try to wrack my brain and remember something I had read on premature labor. At thirty-six weeks, the baby has a good chance of survival. *The lungs, what about the lungs, brain?* Fuck, oh yes, the lungs may be underdeveloped.

How is that helping right now? There's no doubt about it, I'm panicking at the thought of her losing the baby, of losing Charlie.

This isn't Chelsea.

I'm fighting with everything I have to save her. "Okay, listen to me, we'll get through this. Do you have a blanket in the car?"

"In the back... don't leave me, Julian. I'm so scared." Charlie pulls my arm with the only strength she has left.

"Shh... I'll quickly go get it."

In record speed, I run down the hill to fetch the blanket, knowing there's a chance the car could explode at any moment. I spot the blanket lying on the back seat. With the doors unable to open, I grab the rock beside my foot and smash the glass. Reaching in, I feel the jagged glass pierce my skin, but it doesn't stop me from pulling the blanket through. I see a bottle of water and fetch that as well. With contents in hand, I run as fast as humanly possible up the hill and back to Charlie.

I see the calm set in her eyes until she clutches onto her stomach and screams in agony. The contractions are only two minutes apart. *Oh God. Where the fuck is that miracle?* I've never believed in God after Chelsea was taken away, but if anyone can make a miracle happen right now, it has to be the Lord Almighty.

Moving her hair away from her face, I examine the cut

just below her hairline. It's not too deep and shouldn't be my biggest concern. It's the baby now that needs saving.

"I need Lex... I need my husband..." she wails.

My heart aches as she calls *his* name, but she needs *him*, and I need to get *him* here along with an ambulance—anything to save Charlie.

"I'll try to call him, Charlie."

I yank my cell from my pocket, ignoring the poor signal as she whispers his number in short breaths. The phone rings out. I try again. I try ten fucking times until it picks up.

"Who the fuck is this, and what the hell do you want?" he answers coldly.

"Charlie... she's been in an accident..." The crackling overpowers the phone.

"Charlie, what?" he yells.

"Charlie's been in an accident!" The phone dies.

I need to reassure her—the stress isn't helping the baby. The longer the baby stays inside, the better.

"Okay, listen to me... Charlie, you need to try and remain as calm as possible. 9-1-1 will track my cell, and I'm sure Lex will, too. They'll be here shortly. We need to keep your baby calm, okay?"

She nods, understanding it's the only thing we can do right now. I can see her eyes close, the fatigue overpowering her.

"Talk to me, Charlie. Tell me about when Amelia was born. Tell me about some of your happiest memories."

I'm pulling out all the stops. She needs to remain conscious. If she doesn't get through this, neither will I. She nods again, faintly. I hold her hand, trying to maintain contact with her, so she won't fall asleep.

"I was terrified when Amelia was born because I had already lost a baby, Lex's baby. I didn't want to have to go through that again. Lex was calm... he was so calm. My grandmother came to me... she was there and told me everything was going to be okay. But she's not here now, Julian. I don't see her."

Lex's baby? Okay, now isn't the time to delve into her history, but fuck me every which way, this now explains her ties with him.

"I see Chelsea a lot, too."

My voice is quivering as I realize that this is it, this is going to lift the huge burden weighing on my shoulders. My heart, soul, every ounce of my being is caught up in a tangled mess as that déjà vu feeling consumes me. The image of paramedics arriving, the body bag being wheeled in front of me. Her parents arriving at the scene and hearing their excruciating screams surrounding us as they fought with the police officers and begged to see their daughter.

"She was the girl I fell in love with, but she died. Sometimes I see her... she talks to me. She watches over me like an angel. Yet, in my darkest times, I don't see her, and I predict my death."

I wipe away the tear escaping her eyes. "I know you're scared, Charlie, but just because you can't see her doesn't mean your life is over. Tell me something else, tell me about your happy place?"

It's a textbook question—positive thoughts lead to a positive outcome.

"Lex is my happy place... Lex and Amelia. They are my family. They are my reason for living. Amelia started playgroup with my nephew, Andy, a few days ago. She loves the interaction with the kids so much. Lex was upset that she just walked away from us... not even a wave or a backward glance." She lets out the smallest of laughs. "He's so good with her. I never doubted for a moment that he'd be a good father, but to see with my own eyes how much he loves her? I could have a dozen more kids. I love him so much. I don't want to leave him alone in this world..." She sobs, and there's no stopping her.

"Charlie, you won't. We'll get through this, and before you know it, you'll be back in his arms and back at home with your family," I say the words, stunned at my selfless act, confused where it's coming from.

"Julian... I'm sorry..."

"Shh, Charlie. Think about your future. Think about your family."

As I continue to talk, she lets out a terrified scream. *"The baby is coming..."*

"Charlie, look at me," I beg.

Her chocolate-brown eyes stare back at me, rasping breaths follow as her moaning becomes louder. I want to erase her pain, take it all away and bring back the beautiful, strong, and confident Charlie I've grown to know and love.

I want to see her smile.

I want to see a glow spread over her face.

And there's nothing more I want than for her to make more happy memories.

Even if it's without *me*.

I have to be honest, she needs to help me help her, or chances are this baby and Charlie won't survive.

"There's a chance you may have the baby, but I promise you, I'll do everything I can to help you, okay?"

She is breathing heavily, and I can see she's writhing in pain. I open the bottle and hand it to her to drink. She takes small sips but lets out a loud cry as another contraction hits.

"I need to... need to push..." she stutters.

"Charlie, I know this isn't how you imagined having this baby. But I need you to focus—"

My words are cut off as her scream echoes through the night, the wildlife terrified, all flying the coop. I hold her hand, not knowing what the fuck I need to do. Okay, remember when Josie was in the hospital? No, moron, you were in the waiting room and were only twelve years old. Fuck, honestly.

"Julian... I feel the head..."

Even in the cool night, the sweat is dripping off my forehead. I position myself between her legs. Babies come out of vaginas, right? *Where else do they come out of, moron?* It's not like I haven't seen her before. *Oh my God, shut up, head!*

"Okay, Charlie. I'm ready if you need to push, okay? I have a blanket here. And squeeze my hand if you need to."

Charlie grabs my hand and squeezes so damn hard I feel my knuckles crack. She sucks in air, then lets out a loud wail followed by a tiny whimper. I look down and feel my eyes bulge out in disbelief.

Holy fuck, it's a baby's head.

"Okay, Charlie, one more push. You can do this. I see the head."

My heart is pounding in my chest, but I try to ignore it, slowing down my breathing remembering what I need to do. With silent prayers, I pray to the Lord above to bless Charlie and this child with a full life ahead of them. Should he need to take someone, take me, I'm not worthy of being here.

There's no warning. She grabs on tight again, and this time I focus on the baby, trying to guide it out gently with my spare hand. Charlie leans her head forward, squeezing my hand so tight while releasing a gut-wrenching scream. My hand barely catches the baby, the speed of which surprises me as the baby lets out ragged cries. Quickly, I wrap it up while Charlie stares at the tiny baby in awe. I see

Charlie's eyes flutter, causing my familiar panic to reappear.

The blood.

The screaming.

The umbilical cord is still attached.

I shake Charlie slightly to keep her conscious and hand her the baby.

"Look, Charlie... it's your baby."

"My baby..." she mumbles, eyes closing. "My baby is alive?"

"Yes, and it's beautiful."

Charlie is beaming despite her exhaustion, barely able to keep her eyes open or focused. "Is it a boy or a girl?"

Gee idiot, you could've checked that. I look beneath the blanket, a little confused by the cord. "It's a baby girl... you have yourself a beautiful baby girl."

She smiles, but I see the light fading.

I continue to talk, ramble, whatever. "Look, she has your brown hair, and I think... I see a hint of green eyes. Just like Lex's." The words come out of my mouth, surprising even myself. This child is a blessing. Even though it has his blood running through her veins, witnessing this moment, I'm honored. Yet like a double-edged sword, I know everything I feel for Charlie does not measure up to the love they have for each other. These blessings create an everlasting bond which can't and shouldn't be broken by selfish acts.

And in this moment, I realize my life, my actions are *one big selfish act*.

I continue to watch Charlie interact with her daughter while I hold her against her chest.

Even in her frail state, I'm vulnerable staring at her beauty and everything she represents in my life.

Charlie is everything I want in a woman, everything I

want in a soul mate. But what do you do when that whole life you envisioned, the one wrapped up in that neat little package along with white picket fence and minivan is slipping away from you?

Worse yet, what if you're the one pushing it away?

In the distance, the sound of sirens blare on repeat, the loud annoying noise drawing closer to us. I scream for help, a worthless move considering the noise overpowers my pleas. The lights turn around the bend, and the paramedics slow down, pulling alongside my car.

It's only a matter of moments before I see them run down the hill with their equipment and stretcher, followed by a distressed Lex.

"*Charlotte!*" He falls to the ground, his lips trembling with fear.

Cradling her body in his arms, it takes him a few seconds to realize she's holding the baby to her chest. The lady paramedic asks Lex to move out of the way so she can examine Charlie and the baby. Lex argues but soon realizes his wife and baby need assistance.

The male paramedic is kneeling on the ground assessing Charlie's laceration. He turns his head to ask me what happened.

"I saw the car in the ditch and found her inside. She told me she crashed because she had a contraction." I continue on with a shaky voice, "I found her in the car, but I couldn't open the door. Her head was bleeding, but it was a superficial cut. I asked her if she could move all her body parts, and she said yes, so I gently moved her through the trunk as I was paranoid the car would explode."

My heart is heavy at the thought.

Someone was watching over *us*.

"She said the baby was coming, but I could see she was

blacking out, so I kept talking to her to keep her conscious, and then she pushed, and the baby came out."

The lady gives me a sympathetic smile. "You did well. Most people would panic in this situation. The best thing you could've done was keep her conscious."

The paramedic cuts the umbilical cord, and, with caution, they lift Charlie onto the stretcher. She cries for her baby, begging to take it with her. The paramedics explain to her that they need to get to the hospital and make sure both she and the baby are fine. They need to be under observation for the next forty-eight hours.

I watch Lex, distraught as he clutches for Charlie's hand and reassures her everything is going to be fine.

And this moment becomes the hardest part, the moment my heart bleeds again, the moment I'm tortured by my inability to control my emotions, to find any part of me worth the air I am breathing.

The weak smile on my face, a mask I wear, pretending everything will be okay.

She'll be okay with her family.

I'll be okay on my own.

They are walking up the hill, but Lex turns to face me. I wait for his questions.

There are no words, just a look of anguish before he turns back around and climbs into the ambulance with Charlie.

I watch them drive away, and on the side of the road, in the dark night, my tears fall, and I drop to my knees.

It's officially over.

ELEVEN

I have no idea how I made it home.

I'm paralyzed with a numbing feeling, one acting like a shield erasing tonight's events, tonight's nightmare. The fear and terror of watching Charlie almost die in front of my eyes is replaying in my head, then that confusing thought *of* what if I didn't go to see her? Did this wrong move make it right? Screw the fate bullshit, someone was watching over Charlie. She had angels swarming over her like paparazzi, and so it should be. If anyone deserves to stay on this earth, it's Charlie.

Me, I'm scum in the lowest form. I don't deserve anything, especially Charlie.

As I turn the key to my apartment, I hear voices. I don't need this, not now. All I want to do is head straight to the shower and then to bed, leaving Tristan to his own devices.

Walking through the apartment, I see Tristan sitting on the couch with a familiar blonde. They are laughing and enjoying pizza and beer. He sees me, and his expression changes. Concern, pity—yeah, I'm worthless. Kill me now.

"You look like shit, but hey, meet Claudia." Tristan introduces the familiar-looking blonde with very big tits.

Very, very big tits. *No fucking way!*

She looks at me, puzzled, then it clicks. "Julian?"

I muster up the tiniest of smiles, and I mean it's not even a smile, more like a this-is-awkward glare. I really don't need this shit right now.

"How do you know each other?" Tristan asks suspiciously.

I have no excuse, I'm too exhausted even to comprehend my actions. "Uh... we met at a bar. Listen, nice seeing you again. I'm beat, see you in the morning, Tristan."

I don't even wait for a reaction before I head to the shower where I stand there stagnant, no emotion, nothing but emptiness, trying so hard to wash it all away. I sit down on the tiles, back against the wall, letting the water fall against my skin. The tears are solid, becoming deep sobs causing my chest to ache in a way I have never felt before. I open my eyes enough to see my skin wrinkly from so much time spent under the water.

Making my way out, I wrap a towel around me, ready to head to bed. Sleep—my only salvation.

Opening the bathroom door, I see Tristan standing in the middle of the hallway with his bag. His fallen face turns to disgust as he sees me exit.

I really don't need this.

"I'm fairly certain I know how you know Claudia, and you're a fucking jerk. You knew she was my girlfriend."

"Listen, kid, I had no idea—"

"Bullshit! It's like you have no fucking idea how to deal with your own mess of a life, so you have to ruin it for others."

I'm looking for sympathy, trying to keep my voice down. "Look, I've had a terrible night—"

"What? You get busted for stalking your ex?"

Silence.

"I don't need this." I turn my back.

"Maybe you do need this. You're wasting your life. What the hell happened to you, huh? I used to look up to you and just look at you. You're just a huge fucking disappointment. Why the fuck are you so jaded?"

"I don't need to answer to anyone."

"Yeah, well, neither do I." Tristan picks up his bag.

"Where do you think you're going?" I sound parental. This isn't what I signed up for.

"I'm staying with Eric. You need to sort yourself out, Julian. There's only one road you're heading down, and I'm telling you, it's a dead end." He stops by the kitchen counter and throws me an envelope. "And here, an eviction notice." He slams the door behind him.

I am officially alone.

After tonight's events, there's nothing I want to do more than climb into a hole and rot away, but instead, I head to my medicine cabinet and find my sleeping pills.

Sleeping pills or call my dealer.

For tonight, the pills win, but for how much longer?

Frankly, I have no idea.

The room is dark, the light fighting its way in.

The urge, the craving, it devours me.

Alone, I hear the gentle tap on my door, gentle, yet it startles me.

I jump anxiously. It's the monster who lurks under my bed, but he's on the other side of the door.

Like a frightened child, I open it and succumb to the power he holds over me.

He opens his hand, and I see the light illuminating the dark walls. My senses, there's a frenzy within me, taunting and teasing me, and the more it consumes me, I feel myself weaken.

I hand over the last of my money—my rent money.

And like a thief in the night, he disappears.

And I'm alone again with the devil laced in white.

It's all I have now.

No Chelsea.

No Charlie.

And I need to survive, don't I?

I'm like venom. I hurt those around me, including myself.

I walk to the table and lay the white lace carefully in a line. I know the drill. I think about it every second of every day.

I lean down, inches away from euphoria sweeping over me. But I feel a touch, a brush of a hand over my shoulder. I'm hallucinating, I know I'm alone. I bend down again, and the feeling repeats.

I don't look behind me. Instead, I close my eyes allowing my senses to focus.

There's a cool breeze in the room, but the windows are shut.

"In the darkness, our savior will find us. It will drive us into the light."

The voices, I hear them.

"In our weakness of times, find the strength, it lurks

behind the shadows, but it's watching, it is waiting to be asked for help."

I have officially gone crazy.

"Those who live in the light only know the truth to living in the darkness. I am here, I'm watching over you, I am guiding you. Be still, hear my words. The fallen will continue to fall without a savior amongst them."

I listen, and the voices disappear.

My chest is heavy.

Chelsea's voice, without a shadow of a doubt, is echoing in my ear.

I grab the white lace in my hand and walk over to the kitchen, emptying the contents in the sink and scrubbing my hands with scolding hot water until they are red and raw.

But the pain is nothing compared to what my heart feels.

And with that, I sink to the floor with the tears swallowing me whole, the sobs achingly loud, and I scream her name just like I did on the night of the fire.

TWELVE

The wood panels of the door become a big blur as I stay stagnant, gathering my thoughts.

What am I going to say? And why the hell do I need to say anything? Because he's your nephew, and you're the biggest douche for hurting your family.

I decide not to call ahead in case he won't talk to me. I wouldn't talk to me right now. My finger gently presses the buzzer, and the sounds of 'La Cucaracha' echo in the background.

Only Eric would have a doorbell like that.

Relief washes over me when Eric is the one to open the door. I don't, however, appreciate his sympathetic gaze. Sure, I look like roadkill, and there's a chance I smell like it, too. If anyone is going to give me grief about my appearance, it will be Eric.

"Hey, Batman," Eric greets with a small smile. "I'll just grab him."

Eric walks away, and I stand uncomfortably in the living room taking in my surroundings. Eric, being Eric, definitely knows what style means. His apartment is decorated like a photoshoot from a Martha Stewart book. I actually see a picture of Martha Stewart in a frame against a back wall. I want to laugh, but it doesn't quite connect with my face.

There's a white leather sofa smothered with a million pillows perfectly positioned—different colors, textures, and oriental patterns. Looking around, I notice more oriental pieces. He's true to his heritage, even a Buddha is sitting on a floating shelf. There are other ornaments surrounding it and a line of books sitting between bookends. On closer inspection, the bookends are of two male statues doing it doggy-style. *Where on earth does he find this shit?*

There's a creak in the room. I turn around to see Tristan, who's avoiding eye contact with me. I couldn't feel any smaller right now. What kind of a fucking role model am I?

"Hey, mate." Jesus, the nerves are coming out.

He remains quiet, then clears his throat. "Channeling your inner Aussie?"

"I'm trying here. Look, I had no idea. I'd never intentionally sleep with someone you were seeing," I confess.

"I'm not pissed. Well, I was pissed. You can have her."

"Tristan, it was a one-time thing. I'm not after a serious relationship. I've got a lot of things I need to work through."

His eyes meet mine, and just like in Eric's, I see pity. "I know, and I don't know what to say. I'm sorry, too. Maybe I could've done something to help you."

"Well, I'm glad you didn't. Charlie wouldn't be alive if you had stopped me."

"You really loved her, didn't you?" he asks.

I hesitate. "I did. I do. Just not the way she deserves." It's the God-honest truth. "So, when are you coming back home?"

He places his hands in his pockets and rocks back and

forth. "I'm kinda hoping I can bum here until Eric kicks me out."

It's a small kick in the gut, a much-deserved one. I kind of got used to him being around despite my constant complaining.

"Sure, just don't be a stranger, okay? I'm gonna miss your damn PlayStation." I chuckle.

"Yeah, maybe... I might be back soon. It hasn't been unpacked. Eric says part of the roommate agreement is no electrical devices that don't have the intention of getting you off." Tristan rolls his eyes.

Eric yells from the balcony, "I heard that eye-rolling!"

"I better go." My face softens as I attempt to walk away.

In a sudden move, Tristan pulls me into a hug. It's exactly what I need, a small reminder that maybe there are people who do care about me. Maybe I need to stop being a self-absorbed asshole and open my eyes to see that others around me need attention. *The world doesn't revolve around you, Julian Baker, and the quicker you figure that out, the quicker you can go live your life.*

Patting him on the back, acknowledging his kind gesture, I pull away and head toward the door, but not before Eric yells again, "By the way, you look like shit. And it wouldn't hurt you to take a shower. Sheesh!"

With Tristan gone, I'm able to take some leave from work and bury myself in my manuscript. Two weeks of living on cheap packet noodles and coffee. Showering is unheard of, even after Eric's caustic outburst, and I've grown this beehive beard. At first, it irritated me, but I soon got over it, and now I swear, bees could nest in there.

With money running low, or should I say non-existent, I canceled my gym membership and reverted to running through the neighborhood each morning and night to burn off the frustration I'm feeling. I ignore visiting any place where there's a chance of running into Charlie. On the plus side, I'm meeting new people like the old lady down the road who offers me a glass of homemade lemonade every time I run past. Not wanting to be rude as well as being extremely thirsty, I take her up on her offer, and homemade lemonade soon becomes baked shortbread moving onto chicken pot-pie. Needless to say, I'm well-fed, and noodles soon became a distant memory.

Late one morning, I hit send, and the email is officially sitting in Mr. Grimmer's inbox. Leaning my back against the chair, I crack my knuckles one by one in an attempt to relieve the tension. Thirty hours straight with no sleep, so to say I'm exhausted is an understatement. The worst part is that somewhere in the past twenty hours, I realized I hadn't gotten laid in what seemed like forever and hadn't even thought about jerking off, until now.

Clean slate. Just unadulterated raw sex, no names, and no identities. Grabbing my phone, I type in the URL until the page is smothered with every fantasy possible. Clicking on the girl-on-girl porn, I watch for a few minutes attempting to stroke myself but with no relief.

An hour later, it feels like mission impossible until I stumble on a Brazilian gangbang and gee was she in for a special treat with the ten guys hovering over her.

Exactly one minute and ten seconds is all it takes.

Now I'm spent.

I start to doze off until an annoying sound chimes, startling me from my slumber. I'm tempted to ignore it, but thinking it could be Mr. Grimmer, I reach to the floor where I left my laptop last and pull it up to my face to read.

Charlie: *Hi Julian, hope all is well. I would love to*

catch up with you just to say thank you for every-
thing you did for me, if that's ok. Would you be able
to meet us at a park this afternoon? Charlie xx

It's the last person I expected, and it's testing my strength. I'm finally moving on, not to mention she used the word 'us.' Lex won't allow her to see me, and surely if he did, he'd hover over us like a vulture ready to feed on a carcass. There's a part of me, however small it may be, that feels like I owe her this. Whether it's closure, gratitude, whatever the fuck you want to call it, and with that in mind, I text back agreeing to meet. It's only seconds later she responds with a time and place.

And, two hours later, I'm sitting on a park bench, showered and shaved. The beard would scare the children, and it isn't like I'm trying to impress Charlie. Waiting in anticipation, my hands begin to feel clammy, the sun not helping my cause.

Children are darting in and out of the playground, oblivious to anything happening around them. It makes me think about children, family, that whole marriage bullshit. I'm thirty fucking three, and time is wearing thin to start a family. Not to mention, meeting a woman who I want to share my life with. It's a life I'm not sure I want anymore, yet it's flashing before my eyes—what I could be missing out on? Reality hits a few moments later when I get hit in the head with some action figure which a kid throws in the air.

Perhaps that annoying little shit should learn how to act in public.

Yeah, maybe I'm not missing out on anything after all.

At first, I hear the voices, forcing me to look in that direction. Charlie is only a few feet away, pushing one of those strollers which looks like a hovercraft. As I suspected, she's not alone. Lex is standing behind her, watching me with an uncharted look. He bends down to kiss Charlie on the cheek and walks away, tailing his daughter who has run off to the swings.

Charlie welcomes me with a warm smile, taking a seat beside me on the park bench. She's wearing a pair of shorts and a shirt with DC characters on it. Tristan and Charlie would have a lot in common. She continues to smile, and it's impossible to ignore the glow illuminating her beautiful skin. I can't thank the Lord enough. She looks healthy. *Alive.*

Remember, that's what you wanted, to walk away with Charlie alive and happy.

"Hey." She grins.

Charlie appears to be nervous, fidgeting with a loose hem fraying on her shorts. It only lasts a few moments before the baby lets out a wail, distracting Charlie from our awkward silence. With ease, she gently picks up the baby from the stroller and cradles her in her arms. The wailing becomes softer, and without too much intervention, the girl is settled and quiet.

I manage to muster up what I can. Lex's stare stops me from anything further.

"So, this is her?" I keep my expression to no more than a faint smile.

Charlie beams as she talks about her daughter. "This is Ava Lily Edwards."

"She's grown so much, a beautiful girl. I'm really happy for you."

"That means a lot to me, Julian." She pauses as if she's choosing her words carefully. I know Charlie well, she's outspoken, and at times, she and Eric are like two peas in a pod. She is known for being blunt, yet still knows the meaning of tact and manners, unlike Eric, who was born with the verbal-diarrhea gene.

"The reason I called you is that both Lex and I want to thank you..." Her eyes are drawn to him as she says his name, and the connection between them is indisputable. It's almost like you can see a magnetic force pulling them to each other. I'm not completely immune to jealousy, yet I know where I stand with Charlie, and that's not by her side as her husband and father to her children. What the hell am I doing here, rubbing a bottle of salt in a wound? And I mean, of gigantic proportions. They are a happy family, I get it. And I'm a nobody.

She continues to speak, "I know Lex may not show it, but he's as thankful as am I that you saved us. I don't care what you were doing, Julian. All I care about is that this little girl survived and without you... it wouldn't have happened."

The twisting pain in my stomach returns along with that feeling of not knowing whether to be remorseful for my actions or grateful for my mistakes.

Lex is standing at the swings, pushing his daughter. His eyes are watching me, a mixed look of bewilderment and frustration before he turns away and continues to push his daughter. He doesn't look like he wants to kill me, but he doesn't wear a smile either.

"Julian, I know what I did in the past was wrong. I shouldn't have treated you the way I did. Things should've ended with you before I got involved with Lex. I don't regret the outcome... I just wish people hadn't been caught in the crossfire in the process."

"Charlie, it's done. We've moved on." Simple words. I am a man, after all. Women, however, need to elaborate on their feelings like they're writing a novel or something.

"I know, Julian, but despite all that... I think you need help."

I can hear the sincerity in her voice. She has obviously been thinking about approaching me. I know first-hand it's never easy to host an intervention, let alone be on the receiving end. Of course, I need help. I just don't know how to get it.

Allowing myself to absorb her words, I continue to watch the children playing around me. Her daughter, Amelia, has now left the swings and made friends with a boy sitting in the sandpit. All is well until another boy enters the area and catches her attention. She forgets about boy number one, turns her back to him, and begins to build sandcastles with the new boy.

Like mother, like daughter.

"I say that as someone who loves you. Maybe not the way you want to be loved, but I genuinely love you for everything you have done for me. It hurts me to see you hurting. I want to see you live your life and be happy. You deserve the best."

Hearing Charlie say she loves me is enough for me to realize that this part of my life is well over. I can sit and dwell—more like sit and snort—or move on and create a new life for myself away from Charlie and the temptations that lurk around me.

The conversation is short-lived as Amelia runs toward us. She's wearing a Batman T-shirt with a cape plus little black gumboots and is covered in sand. She doesn't seem to care, though. What is it with kids and sandpits?

"Mommy! Can I take baby Ava on the swings?"

Charlie touches her cheek, a motherly gesture that doesn't go unnoticed. "Buggy, she's too little. Why don't you call Daddy over?"

Great. Showdown.

"I'm not Buggy anymore. I'm Batman! See, look at my cape."

The irony. If it weren't for her emerald green eyes and everything about her face that mirrors Lex's, you could seriously question her paternity.

Charlie lets out a small giggle. "Yeah, I know what you're thinking."

Her laugh is infectious, and I can't help but laugh along with her. "So, she likes Batman?"

"Uh-huh, been obsessed with him ever since she saw him at her cousin's birthday last year. She's a crazy one. She keeps ladybugs as pets. Had like twenty of them in her room, hence, why she got the name 'Buggy.' We thought having a daughter meant tea parties and an overload of pink, but let me tell you, it's been everything but." Charlie's smile remains fixed. Even though her daughter may be a tomboy, you can see the proud look on her face. "Eric even bought her this fancy kids' tea set from London for her birthday. She opened the present and ran off to find Rocky because his present to her was a basketball. She loves to watch the Lakers play."

"I can only imagine Eric would've been devastated," I respond at ease.

"Gutted doesn't even cover it. I believe he dropped the F-bomb, and let me tell you, Amelia repeats what you say, so Eric got an earful from us that night."

We laugh for a little while longer before Lex walks over to us. He stands beside Charlie, taking baby Ava off her and moving his lips to her forehead. I see Charlie watch him in awe, but her eyes do this thing as if she's trying to get him to say something.

We all remain silent, only the sounds of the children

screaming and the occasional rustle in the trees from a slight breeze can be heard. The clouds have formed into a cluster, the shades of gray warning us of what's to come. In the distance, a roar of thunder startles the children, and parents scramble to collect their family and belongings before the rain.

For me, there's a different kind of storm brewing, and it's about to strike.

Lex clears his throat. "You saved my wife and my baby."

It's not a thank you, more of a statement.

I don't say a word.

Charlie places her hand on mine, and the touch makes me ache. "Thank you, Julian. Give yourself that. Despite whatever your intention was, you saved us."

I look directly into her eyes, watching her stare back at me. She stands and leans in to embrace me.

My strength, my weaknesses, every emotion possible is swirling in my head, and not wanting to linger in this moment, I pull away and give her the smile she deserves.

Lex continues to stand beside her, watching us intently.

"Thank you," he murmurs.

It's as clear as day.

I give them all a final smile before walking away for good.

Another chapter in my life closed.

But this part of the book ended happily for them, not me. I still have a lot of soul-searching to do.

I no longer have Chelsea, I no longer have Charlie, and I refuse to die in a heap of white acid.

But I do need help.

Who's going to save me now?

THIRTEEN

I shuffle my legs in an attempt to get comfortable. Whoever invented plastics chairs is a dickhead. Perhaps it's not even the chairs, more the fact that I'm sitting in a circle surrounded by complete strangers who, just like me, are sitting on these shitty plastic chairs. On one side of me is my baggage, and on the other, my demons. *Is there a savior in the room?* That's why we all sit here praying that someone will save us from our inevitable death.

The support meeting is located in a quiet hall behind one of our local churches. I think fate stepped in when I stumbled upon the small ad in the newspaper. I didn't want some big-shot rehab facility. Call me naïve, but I'm not that fucked-up.

An older lady with gray-streaked hair sits down and smiles at each of us. She looks at peace, and there's a calm aura surrounding her. I don't want to stare at anyone, but curiosity gets the better of me. We're all puppets in this freak show. Maybe I'm not so screwed-up, or worse yet, maybe I'm the most insane person sitting in this room.

Something tells me the tranny sitting across from me has bigger issues.

The lady clears her throat, and on closer inspection, she has a Bible in her hand.

"Good afternoon, friends." Her voice is soothing. She reminds me a lot of my grandmother. "My name is Hazel, and I'd like to welcome our new friend."

There are a few smiling faces in the group, and then there are those staring blankly into space.

"I'd like to tell you about myself and why I am here today." She takes a deep breath. I sense I'm not going to like what she's going to say. "Twenty years ago, in front of this building, I lost my husband and son."

An eerie silence falls over the room. The tranny is clutching a handkerchief, dabbing each eye, careful not to smear the excessive amount of blue eye shadow smeared across his eyelids.

"We had just finished Sunday morning mass and were walking out of the church to our car. My son stopped to tie his shoe, and my husband waited for him. I was only a few feet ahead when I heard the loud bang. The next minute, I see my husband and son lying on the ground." Hazel traces her fingers along the engraved crucifix that sits on the cover of the Bible. "It was a boy who took my family away from me. He was only thirteen years old, bullied into a gang, and he did what he needed to do to survive on the streets. I have spent so many years asking why I was punished, why would God take away my family? The pain comes in waves, but somehow I have to find purpose in why I was spared."

My heart is breaking for her. To have your husband and son shot in front of you is unthinkable.

"I'm not here to preach the Lord, despite that I carry this around." She lifts the Bible, closing her eyes for a brief moment. "This is my way of finding peace. Everyone is different, and that's the first step to healing."

A man sitting beside her is rocking back and forth. He scratches himself, annoyed, and Hazel recognizes his impatience. His hair is ginger-colored and covers his face, so his eyes are barely seen. He's wearing brown baggy jeans and a dull green T-shirt. It's an inappropriate moment to be thinking that he looks like Shaggy from *Scooby-Doo*, but he sure does.

"I still haven't found it, Hazel," he complains.

Hazel smiles at the man. I suspect this isn't the first time she's heard this.

"Jerry," she softly scolds. "You have found that first step, you just need to accept it."

He continues to be irritated, scratching like a madman. Something about his scratching is contagious. Soon I find myself scratching my arms like I have chickenpox.

"I need to get the hell out of here," he huffs.

Hazel walks over and places her hand around Jerry's shoulder. At first, he flinches, then his body visibly relaxes.

What the fuck was that about?

A slight creak of the door interrupts whatever the hell just happened with Jerry. A woman sneaks in and sits at a chair near the exit. We all turn to her direction, though with her head bowed down and face covered by a hood, we can't see her face. Hazel looks pleased, although the woman does not look up.

I can't help but watch her. It's boiling hot outside and, in this room, so why is she wearing a hoody? A part of me is hoping she'll look my way, but nothing. I give up and focus my attention on Hazel and the rest of the group.

An older man, perhaps late sixties, pipes up, "My name is Fred."

"Hi, Fred," everyone greets in unison.

"It was 1992, the Barcelona Olympics. We were celebrating the US winning gold, and a bunch of us holiday folk were crossing a busy street to get to the local bar. As we crossed the road, this taxi comes out of nowhere, and I watch it, frozen in the middle of the road. My friend pushes me out of the way, saving me from my death." Fred falls into a digestive silence, his story appearing to be more tragic than his near brush with death. "I have agyrophobia, the fear of crossing roads," he admits.

"At first, it wasn't a huge deal, but as time went on, I struggled to go to work, out for groceries, or even just visit my neighbor across the street. My wife ended up leaving me and took my daughter with her. She'd had enough of my paranoia." The sad tone in his voice only mildly projects the turmoil he's facing and the bitter disappointment in himself for losing his family—the poor man.

"Fred, last week you told us about your journey to the local store by foot," Hazel says encouragingly.

Fred stares at the floor, nervously clicking his scuffed brown boots together. "Yeah, I walked, but I stood watching the store from across the street for an hour."

So many questions run through my mind. How on earth does he get anywhere? Is it even possible not to cross a road? My fear of coyotes seems so insignificant right now.

"I know what you new folk must be thinking... how do I get anywhere? Well, I drive. If I have to go to the post office across the road, I get in my car and drive."

Jerry mumbles something under his breath starting a heated debate with Fred.

Not paying attention to either of them, I find myself drawn to the mystery girl who continues to sit in silence near the door. From what I can see of her face, she is quite pale. Her cheekbones are prominent and not in a healthy way. Although she's wearing loose articles of clothing, her frame appears to be emaciated. I don't want to stare, but there's something about her that intrigues me.

"Honestly, you two fight like cats and dogs. Grow some balls and shut up already." The tranny has had enough of their bickering. He, she, hell I don't know, is wearing a low-cut dress with a visible bust. My instincts would say 'he' due to his Adam's apple that's practically jumping out at me.

Stop fucking staring.

"Like you're one to talk, Penny," Jerry mocks. "If I need balls, I'm sure you've still got a pair tucked into your panties."

"Jerry, Penny," Hazel softly calls their names and, like magic, they shut up, although still angry from their argument. I suspect Hazel is the mother hen to everyone in this room. They seem to respect her, and the calming influence she has over them is likely the exact reason they come back every week. "I always like to give individuals a task to take home with them, a step to healing. I want you to focus on one thing that made you smile this week. It could be a delicious ice cream you ate or maybe someone you saw. Something or someone who makes you happy, even for just a moment." Hazel smiles hopefully at each of us.

"Does having sex with a cab driver count?" Penny sighs dreamily.

"What is it with you and sex? I swear, Penny, sometimes you're such a wh—" Jerry is interrupted by a furious Penny.

"A what, Jerry? A whore? Just because I like sex doesn't make me a whore!"

Whoa! We have entered some awkward territory now.

"Stop being such a jerk in front of our new member,

Jerry." Penny looks directly at me and shoots me a wink. Jerry rolls his eyes.

"Thank you... Penny?" I ask politely.

"Yes, Penny... Penny Tration." She bats her eyelashes at me this time.

I shake my head unable to hide my smile, and obviously, I'm not the only one as Fred is bowing his head with a smirk on his face.

"Nice to meet you, Penny Tration." I hold in my laughter as best as I can. "My name is Julian... Julian Baker."

The sound of a chair screeching along the wooden floor echoes through the room. My head turns to the noise coming from the hooded girl. She lifts her head slightly, and I'm eager to see her face. Only her lips are visible, a pale pink with the right corner raw from where she's been chewing, most likely due to the anxiety of this meeting.

What the fuck is it about her?

Whatever it is needs to stop right here, right now. I came here to heal and find peace, not to hook up and sleep with someone in the group. Next time I sit in this chair, I'm almost certain it will be my turn to open the vault of my past and lay it bare for everyone to see.

It terrifies me to the core.

As if Hazel can sense my trepidation, she casually walks over and places her palm over mine. "Don't be afraid. It'll happen when you're ready."

"I think I'm ready, I just... I don't know," I blurt out.

"Julian, dear boy, you'll know when you're ready to speak. Your heart and mind will be in sync. Don't force yourself."

My heart and mind need to be in sync.

Repeat, *my heart and mind need to be in sync.*

FOURTEEN

I slam my laptop shut.

My frustration and anxiety over not receiving a response from Mr. Grimmer has sent me into a spiral of self-doubt. Fuck that no-news-is-good-news bullshit. No news means I'm a big fat failure, and my dreams, once again, have been flushed down the drain along with my last stash of coke.

It's a quarter to seven in the evening, only fifteen minutes until I have to leave for the weekly meeting. The majority of this week, I spent in the office without any leads, and I'm pretty sure I'll be fired any day now. Considering my paycheck isn't enough to cover my rent, my eviction is inevitable despite convincing the landlord to give me more time. Life sure is one big bowl of roses.

Once again, I find myself sitting in the uncomfortable plastic chair. Note to self—*invent comfortable plastic chairs.* How can you open your mind to healing when your nuts are squashed against your dick and shoved somewhere up your ass?

Hazel walks in and sits down with her Bible in her lap.

She closes her eyes, and I watch as her lips move. Making the sign of the cross, she opens her eyes from what must have been a silent prayer.

Fred walks in and takes his usual seat, followed by Jerry and Penny arguing again. I don't bother to listen to their conversation, assuming they'll air it out for everyone to hear shortly.

Penny takes a seat beside me. Today she's wearing a bright yellow dress that has pictures of candy on it. Her platform pumps painted with the union jack, give her height, and she's towering over everyone in this room. Her hair is bright blue—maybe not hair, more like a wig. I'm disturbing myself with how much attention I am paying to detail.

Hazel welcomes everyone back, but I'm quick to scan the room and see the mystery hooded girl isn't here. I am a little disappointed. I hoped I'd have gotten a glimpse of her face today.

Jerry is profusely scratching and telling everyone he's out of here. Once again, Hazel goes through the motions to calm him.

Fred tells his story *again*.

It's *Groundhog Day*, and I'm Bill Murray.

Perhaps the only thing keeping my attention is Penny trying to pull her dress up above her thigh to entice me.

Scrotum and dick. If you got them, I'm not interested.

Sometime during Fred's story, mystery girl walks in. Her hood is off, and her bright red hair stands out. It's cut short in a bob style with her bangs a longer length falling below her eyes. She continues to wear the black hooded jacket in the sweltering heat. I need to look away before she catches me.

Hazel begins to ask us about how our task went, the one thing that made us happy this week.

Fred is first to answer. "I watched a rerun of *Seinfeld*. It was the episode where George ate an onion. I laughed for an hour. Then my neighbor banged on my door, and we got into an argument, so maybe I shouldn't laugh so much." His smile fades from wry to pensive.

Hazel is quick to praise him. "Fred, laughter is the best medicine. Don't be discouraged by your neighbor's discontent."

Jerry grunts, prompting Hazel to ask him the same question. "Nothing made me happy, except for when I saw this kid fall off a bike. Yeah, maybe then I snickered. Kid deserved it, was showing off and all."

Hazel chooses her words carefully. "Jerry, we talked about seeking joy in others' pain."

"Yeah, so what? Kid thought he was King Shit."

"He's just a child, he has yet to learn the consequences of his actions," Hazel reminds him.

"Big fucking deal. I was a kid, too, okay? Do you think they cared about what they were doing to me?" he answers back in a sinister tone.

"Jerry, who was there to show them right from wrong? They knew no better. Your brothers felt the pain you did, and unfortunately, their way of dealing with the hurt and resentment was to take it out on you."

Jerry pulls his knees to his chest and begins to rock back and forth.

Hazel softens her tone. "We must understand a cycle can be broken. The actions of the past don't need to repeat themselves. We need to look at the whole picture, understand the story and what lies beneath."

She turns to look at me and gives me a slight nod. *Great. It's now or never, right?*

My throat feels dry. God, what I'd do for a scotch on the rocks right now.

"I was sitting in a café. The lady beside me ordered a red velvet cupcake. Reminded me of this woman I was fond of... well, was in love with. At least I thought it was love, I think." My thoughts and words come out jumbled. I sound like a moron.

"I hear hesitation surrounding the word 'love?'" Hazel asks.

"I don't think..." I struggle to get my words out. "I thought I loved Chelsea. She was my neighbor, and I was crazy about her. She'd tease me, taunt me, and I just took anything, any scraps she would throw my way. I was convinced I loved her, but I was seventeen. Who falls in love at seventeen?"

"I fell in love at seventeen... with my hand." Jerry laughs.

Penny slaps her hand on her knee, letting out a huge roar.

"Ignoring your age, what feeling do you remember about her? What feelings do you associate with love?" Hazel's questions leave me stumped.

"She was beautiful. She had long brown hair, the kind that looks like it belongs in a commercial for shampoo. It was so silky and smelled like vanilla. Used to make me weak in the knees every time I was near her." I smile, remembering her fondly, something I haven't done for a long time. "Chelsea was a daredevil, everything I wasn't. It scared me yet excited me at the same time. It would make me so angry when she'd sneak guys home and screw them in her room while her parents were in the living room watching *The Price is Right*."

"Sounds like my kind of girl!" Penny giggles.

"She liked sex, all right. Maybe too much." The knots in my stomach tighten, leaving me slightly out of breath. "The night she died, I told her I loved her...." Bowing my head, I attempt to fight back the pain threatening to invade every part of me. "You should've seen the look on her face. I had never seen that side of Chelsea it was like she was honored. I don't know, I can't explain it, but that face haunts me to this very day."

"Haunts you or eases the pain?" Hazel asks for clarification.

"Both. Sometimes my memory of her face is so clear, and other times I can't remember, and it frustrates me. Those are the times I can only see the flames."

The group is silent for moments on end. *Great, I'm the lunatic in here.*

"It's common for many people to forget the good and remember the bad. It's important that you try to remember as many good things as you can. For instance, I try to remember every Sunday when my family would leave church to head down to the ice cream parlor." She smiles.

"The same church where your family was shot?" Jerry asks in shock.

"Yes. Every Sunday for ten years we walked down that same path, and every Sunday was a joyous occasion until that very last one." Hazel's face doesn't change, and I wonder how she can remain calm while reliving that disturbing memory.

I start to find my voice. "The nightmares plague me, the same scene over and over again. Chelsea driving the car into the tree, and the flames engulfing it before my eyes. The feeling of being helpless, watching her body dragged from the wreckage and hearing the paramedics pronouncing her dead. The only thing that stopped it was a woman I met named Charlie."

There's a cough in the room, but I'm too late to see who it came from.

"Tell us about this Charlie?" Penny places her hand on mine, conflicting me in every which way.

"She looks like Chelsea, beautiful, smart. God, she's perfect."

"And?" Penny waits in anticipation.

"She was in love with someone else. I had no chance."

"Women think with their kitties, I should know, after all." Penny flicks her hair behind her shoulder.

"Honestly, Penny, you're such a—"

"It's getting old, Jerry, much like your outfit," Penny mocks.

I interrupt the both of them. "Charlie isn't like that. She loves him, always loved him. You can't compete if there's no competition to begin with."

"So, then why are you here?" Fred asks.

Million-dollar question. *Why am I here?*

"Because losing Chelsea and Charlie forced me to do drugs. I'm my own worst nightmare. I know I need to find a way to move forward in my life without using people to replace what I lost."

Hazel places her hand on her heart. "My boy, you've just passed that first step, accepting what you need to overcome."

It was exactly like in school, the teacher praising you in front of the whole classroom. Inside I feel the relief wash over me, Penny leaning over to squeeze my hand with delight. Fred begins to clap, acknowledging my achievement. Jerry sulks, as usual, then in a bold move, leans toward me and sticks out his fist. I knock fists with him, weird but okay. Whatever.

My eyes wander over to the mystery girl. With her sleeves up, I can see red marks just above her wrist. There's no mistaking them, some are old scars, and others look raw and new.

They are cuts.

I beg her with my eyes to look in my direction. She's a girl in pain, maybe more so than the rest of us in this room. With every cut that scars her pale skin, I want to mend her and give her the hope she needs. Whatever it is about this girl that pulls me in, I need to control it. Something has a hold of me, and with alarm bells ringing in my head, once again, I have to stop trying to find the next obsession.

Everything comes to a halt when I watch her head lift, and her eyes stare directly at mine.

There's something familiar about them. I've seen them before. I wrack my brain but come up with nothing.

This is a huge fault of mine and exactly what I do every time. I think I see people from the past in my present.

Breaking her gaze, I shake my head, clearing my thoughts.

"Darling, you up for a drink at the bar around the corner? My treat." Penny pulls a twenty out of her cleavage.

I nod and laugh at her antics, only to miss the mystery girl leaving the room, vanishing without a trace.

FIFTEEN

"So, one day, my father catches me dressed in my mother's church clothes parading in front of the bathroom mirror. He beat me to a pulp, leaving me for dead. It was the last time I ever saw that sick bastard."

Penny's horrific life story can only be heard with a bottle of tequila and two shot glasses. There are parts that had me in stitches and others that made me want to wring the neck of the man who brought her into this world.

We have been sitting at the bar, playing a game of 'let's take turns telling our tragic stories' followed by a strong shot of tequila.

"Okay, my turn," I slur.

Penny enjoys being asked questions, unlike me.

"So, what exactly is happening down south? Do you like men or women?"

A laugh escapes her mouth, almost spilling a peanut she's eating. "Don't have the money to get frankenweenie chopped off, and I'm all about the man." She slides closer to me before grabbing my forearm and laughing off her comment. "Sweetie, you're drop-dead gorgeous, and I'm certain that any woman who's been near your ding-dong has been sat... tis... fied." She clicks her fingers, then gracefully pours more tequila into her glass.

"Penny, I'm all about the pussy. No offense." I chuckle.

"Sweetie, no offense taken, but if you need a good whack up your backside, you know where to find me."

The thought made me squirm in pain, not pleasure. I wonder if Eric would be interested. For God's sake, Julian, don't play gay matchmaker. That's such a chick thing to do.

Curbing my curiosity, I ask the question that's been bugging me for days. "So, what the hell is up with you and Jerry?"

"Urgh, he's such an immature little brat who needs a sitting in the naughty corner to think about his actions," she complains.

"What's his story?"

"I'm not certain on the details, only what Fred has told me. He was beaten by his brothers when he was younger. Happened for years, and apparently, they would make him lie to his parents that kids in the neighborhood were doing it. The sick thing was that they would do it in front of other kids to show off. Kinda like a bet." She slams a shot of tequila down, wincing as it burns her throat. "So, one day he was so badly hurt that he was rushed to the hospital. He told his parents everything, but they refused to believe him, so when he was twelve or something, he ran away to live on the streets."

"That's fucked up. How old is he?" I couldn't help but feel sorry for Jerry after Penny's tell-all story.

"I think he's like twenty."

"He looks so much older," I wondered out loud.

"The streets will do that to you. Okay, enough serious

talk, are you up for some fun?" she asks with a devilish grin on her face.

"Sure, Penny Tration, lead the way."

We're sitting at a table with Hazel and a room full of people playing bingo. The last time I played this game was probably in the eighties with my grandparents and their old-folk friends at the nursing home. The only thing that changes is that I'm now full of tequila. Bingo and tequila equal a very entertaining Thursday night. Unlike me, Penny holds her liquor without too much drama. When she yells out bingo, I burst out into a fit of laughter causing everyone to turn and look at me. I'm not sure what's so funny, but I can't stop, and it isn't long before Penny and Hazel join in, which only adds to the hilarity of the situation.

"So, let me get this straight, you were out all night drinking tequila and playing bingo with a drag queen?" Tristan questions, scratching his head in confusion.

"I never said 'drag queen'!" I yell defensively.

"Okay, tranny, then?"

"I don't know, I probably should've asked when it was appropriate to ask," I admit.

"When is it ever an appropriate time to ask that question?" Tristan snickers.

Sitting up from the couch, my head is ready to explode. "When you're playing truth and on your tenth shot of tequila. Anyway, what the hell are you doing here?"

I didn't notice it earlier, but Tristan has two Starbucks cups sitting on the table. I grab one and take a sip, hoping it will cure my pounding head. *Mmm... fresh coffee.*

"Eric's gone to New York for a few days, so I thought why not spend time with my favorite uncle!" He cheers.

"I'm your only uncle," I point out.

"And a great one at that." A cheesy grin is plastered on his face. Not immune to his buffoonery, I shake my head with a smile.

"Aw shucks, kid, nice spiel. Now, what do you want?"

"Nothing." He smirks.

"Okay, so what's been happening at Eric's?"

Tristan's shoulders perk up like a meerkat on watch. "What do you mean? Nothing's happening."

"Geez, don't bite my head off. I'm merely asking how things are going," I huff.

"Sorry. Good. Great. Um... it's fine. Eric is busy a lot with work and stuff."

"Sure. I know when he worked in New York for Charlie, they were inundated with new clients. LA must definitely have its share of work with all the celebrity shit that goes on around here."

"Yeah, he tends to come home late and is such a bitch when he's tired. Take, for instance, last night... I cook this awesome meal, and all he does is complain that he has a headache and then goes straight to bed. I slaved over that meal for hours," he complains.

"You sound like a married couple," I say casually.

"Wh... why would you say that?" He stumbles on his words.

"Because you sound like a married couple... lighten up, kid. Eric has his own life. Don't forget that you're living under his roof."

Tristan stays for the next hour before leaving to attend an audition for some infomercial. It's for some crazy device that cooks meals in less than two minutes. It's laughable, but being a great uncle, I wish him luck.

Again, I find myself alone, anxiously waiting for a response from Mr. Grimmer. If I don't hear anything by the end of the week, I'm going to take the initiative and contact him. This limbo feeling is getting old.

Thursday rolls around, and before I know it, I'm back sitting in the circle of troubles.

Everyone is here, chatting away about last night's episode of *Survivor*, from who is deemed as playing the game to who's making alliances. It's a light-hearted conversation, and even Hazel joins in, not caring the topic has swayed into reality television instead of the power of healing.

Trying my best to stay in the conversation, I anxiously wait for mystery girl to turn up. It's already half an hour into our meeting and nothing. I figure she's given up, perhaps it got too hard. That thought scares me, the harm she could do to herself.

Tonight, Penny opens up about her past, her attempts to contact her family with no luck, life on the streets, and her take on how people react to her lifestyle. It's heartbreaking to hear the pain and ridicule she endures almost every day, yet she has the strongest backbone out of anyone I have ever met. She may have been beaten physically, but mentally, she's as tough as nails.

During her confession about falling in love with a married man, the door creaks, and a body slips through, taking a seat at the back.

Mystery girl.

My eyes wander of their own accord, my brain following like a lost puppy. Today, she's wearing a T-shirt which reads, 'I Like Boys That Sparkle.'

Great, one of those vampire-loving chicks.

Her arms are visible, no jacket or sleeves to cover the scars and cuts. She is very pale, odd for living in California, but maybe she isn't a native or one of those folks who claims they never tan like albinos.

Her fiery red hair is covering her eyes as she continues to bow her head. Scanning the rest of her, I stop at a shiny piece of gold which catches my attention. Nestled on her left hand is a gold band. *She's married.*

Time to back the fuck up. I turn away to clear my mind of the ray of thoughts swirling around. It's not like I'm here to score, so who cares that she's married? What you feel is just genuine concern for someone other than yourself. Her scars are laid bare for all of us to see. What caused them is now piquing your curiosity. That's all.

Penny's loud voice distracts me. "Let's call him 'Mr. X.' So, we were seeing each other for about six months. I thought he was the one. He was confused, I understood that. Pushed into a life he didn't want, married, two-point-four children, white picket fence, drove a Prius."

"A Prius?" Jerry sneers.

"Uh-huh. Like I was saying, he was living this double life. So, one day, he tells me he's leaving all that for me. What's a girl to think? I was over the moon! We had picked out an apartment to rent. He even started bringing things over, and then one day, he vanished."

Fred leans over and pats Penny on the back. "I tried to find him, and according to everyone, he had left town with his family. A year later, I ran into him at the airport, random fluke. He was there with his family and pregnant wife. I was still hurting. Why me? Wasn't I good enough?" Penny cries.

Hazel hands Penny a box of tissues as the tears stream

down her face. Perhaps her strength was masking her weakness. Her sobs are loud, ugly cries.

"Have you thought for a moment how you played a role in ruining this sanctity of marriage?" The voice comes from mystery girl.

She speaks and sounds like she's ready to go to war.

"Of course, but honey, a man tells you he loves you, you take those words to heart. Sometimes your heart won't see or care about anyone else," Penny defends herself.

"Well, even though he's a right prick, he should be thanking his lucky stars he still has his family," mystery girl states angrily. She lowers her head, her words barely audible. "I wonder every day why he was taken from us. I wonder if there's anything I could've done to keep him alive. When I look at my son, I wonder if he feels the pain I do. Sometimes I think I'm healing, but then something happens... his song comes on the radio, someone walks past me with the same hair color. Or even that stupid baby soap ad that comes on where the family is hugging it out."

The group is quiet, allowing her to voice her feelings.

"That baby soap commercial gets me every time," Fred confesses.

Jerry and Penny nod in unison.

She tugs on her shirt to hide the nerves. "What family does my son have? How can a family be just a mother?"

Hazel speaks up, "Family isn't defined by a dad, a mom, and a child. Family is a feeling, not a status. When I lost Richard and George, I asked the same exact question."

"Why didn't you remarry or have more children?" mystery girl questions Hazel.

"I was in my early forties, and having more children wasn't really in the cards for me. As for marriage? I've dated other men. In fact, I've been together with Miles for almost four years now."

"And you don't want to marry him?" Clearly, mystery girl has found her voice.

"Miles and I have a great relationship as it is. He lost his wife to breast cancer a few years back. He has two daughters who I love dearly. For us, we enjoy what we have today. Marriage is sacred, and we took those vows with people who are no longer here. I do love Miles as he loves me."

It's like a vault is being opened, and the questions and curiosity are laid on the table eager to get some sort of answer.

"Do you get jealous when he talks about his wife? I just don't get it. I never want to stop talking about my husband. He was my life... he is my life," mystery girl corrects herself.

"Oh, dear, no. We love to talk about our great loves. It's a part of keeping the memory alive. I've spent a lot of time with his wife's family and enjoy hearing all the wonderful stories. She was a remarkable woman, and I know why Miles loved her dearly. When I see Miles' face light up talking about her, it makes me complete. She'll always be a part of him, and she brings out the best of him. Makes him the person he is today. Understanding the roles people play or played in our lives gives us a sense of comfort and sometimes closure on events that are beyond our control."

Hazel walks over to the girl and puts her hand out. The girl is scared, holding back, but soon places her hand in Hazel's and follows her to our circle where she takes a seat beside her.

I continue to watch her because something is nagging me, this feeling of familiarity, and wracking my brain is getting me nowhere. The group continues to talk about a field trip next Saturday. I pay absolutely no attention because mystery girl is watching me. She continues to stare at me, her bleak eyes shadowed by dark circles. Her eyebrows rise slightly as we continue this game of curiosity.

Around us, everyone stands. I say goodbye, breaking my gaze.

Penny is warning Hazel about her fear of roosters and how if we see one on the field trip, she may piss in her pants —her words, not mine.

"Julian." The voice is beside me, she's so close, her scent of sweet candy lingers around us.

"Yes, nice to meet you... uh?" I extend my hand as a polite gesture, hoping she introduces herself.

"What's wrong, Batman? Cat got your tongue?"

"Okay, you got me there. You look familiar, but hey, my mind could be playing tricks on me. No point hiding the obvious in this group."

"It's like one big fucked-up family in here," she states.

"Yeah, but it kinda makes me feel normal." I wait eagerly, and after only a few moments, she extends her hand and shakes mine.

"Adriana," she says.

"Nice to meet you, Adria—" I cut myself off mid-sentence. "Adriana Edwards?"

"Was, now Evans," she corrects me.

I pull my hand away abruptly, the weight of her identity throwing me into a panic. I mumble something about having to go somewhere before leaving the room in a rush, and I mean a *Roadrunner*-on-steroids kind of rush back home.

Adriana Evans.

Charlie's best friend.

Lex's sister.

Mystery girl is finally revealed.

Standing in front of my building, I look up into the sky, attempting to communicate with the universe. Are you fucking kidding me? What the fuck are you trying to do? The purpose of this group is to forget and move on, but no, you throw someone else into the mix to test me beyond my capability. So, she's off-limits, not that I'm looking for my soul mate at this meeting.

Just stay away from her. You can do this.

I'm so fucking screwed any way I turn. I need to let off steam, something to distract me from this bullshit excuse of a life I'm dealt.

Taking out my cell, I dial her number.

"Hey, doll, booty call?" she teases.

"Bingo call?" I answer, defeated.

"Oh, sweetie, that bad? Be there in ten."

I hang up and walk down the road to the bingo hall, hoping Penny will kick my ass and make me forget about my encounter with Adriana Evans.

SIXTEEN

The last meeting sent a huge curveball up my ass, bouncing every which way. Okay, seriously, too much hanging out with Penny and her ass talk.

Since I wasn't paying attention in the last meeting, I have no idea why on earth we're going on a field trip. Hazel feels that each one of us needs to focus our negative energy into positivity and helping others. Fine, I get that. I just have no idea how I'll face Adriana, and I am perturbed by going backward in this healing process. How can I open up my feelings talking about her best friend? Not to mention how I tried to screw her brother over several times.

Yep, fucking backward, all right.

The last time I sat on a bus was in high school, and fifteen years later, nothing has changed. Still the same uncomfortable seating, my nuts hurting every time we hit a bump in the road, and the saddest part is that I'm thirty-three and riding a bus to go on a field trip.

Even though we have the bus to ourselves, Penny decides to squish in beside me. The entire way, she rambles on and on about how when she was little, a rooster pecked her, leaving an ugly scar that no amount of laser surgery can remove.

"Penny, if you're afraid of it happening again, why do you wear a short, hot pink dress?" I ask.

She smooths the creases in her dress. "Honey, you never know who you might meet at a place like this. I need to look fabulous."

"You have eight-inch heels on."

"And a matching hot pink thong... in case you were wondering."

I let out a laugh before my attention diverts to Adriana. She's sitting alone a few seats before us, staring blankly out the window. Suddenly, I feel terrible for the way I abandoned her that day. She hasn't done anything wrong, apart from sharing the same blood as the man who can only be described as my nemesis.

Thankfully, it's only a short ride because Fred and Jerry get into a heated debate over politics. Jerry is intelligent, something you wouldn't pick up on by looking at him.

When Hazel announces we have arrived, I bolt off the bus desperate for some fresh air. Hazel talks about helping others, and I don't realize she's referring to animals. When I question her choice, she says many people have great difficulty helping other humans, and we need to remember that we aren't the only ones walking this earth.

At the shelter, we assemble ourselves near the entrance. It's a small, run-down building surrounded by acres of land. The sounds of different animals mixed into one are loud enough for us to hear at the entrance. The dominant crow of the rooster startles Penny, causing her to jump behind Jerry lecturing her for her childish behavior.

The manager of the shelter, Amy, welcomes us. Amy tells us why she opened the shelter and the stories of the different animals she rescues. As she takes us on a tour introducing us to each one of her friends, my heart sinks as I listen to what they have endured. Jerry seems annoyed, his usual self. Fred is more compassionate and spends his time with a sick cat and its kittens which were rescued from an abandoned house. Penny is clinging onto Hazel, repeating her story about the rooster. She throws the word 'cock' in there way too much.

Jerry, being Jerry, says he's out of here.

I hear a slight snicker beside me. It's Adriana trying to hide a smile. Smiling back at her, I'm slightly reluctant to be the first to speak.

"You can talk to me, you know. I don't bite," she offers.

"Your shirt read 'I Like Boys That Sparkle,' so I thought you were running with a vampire clan," I respond.

"Ha! I can't think of anything worse... unable to die and living forever?"

There's an underlying truth to that statement, and I know I'm not emotionally strong enough to give a response like Hazel would.

"Julian, Adriana, who do you have here?" Hazel asks as she kneels to look at a dog lying in the cage before us.

Amy walks toward us. "This is Blaze. She's a Labrador. We rescued her from the wildfires a few weeks ago."

I bend down with Hazel to take a look at the poor dog. She is lying on her side, her panting quick, burned on one side leaving a huge scar. Her eyes are dull, no life left in them. The pain appears unbearable, and I ache knowing there isn't anything I can do to take it away.

"Is she okay?" I ask, my words ragged, unable to hide my sorrow.

"We hope she'll recover. We performed surgery to repair her burned tissue. The problem is that when we found her, she was with one of her pups. His name is Ash. The others couldn't be found," Amy says, struggling to choke back her tears.

I see Blaze's pup beside her, nestled into her belly. Unlike a typical puppy, he lacks exuberance and continues to sleep. He's abnormally small for his breed.

Adriana kneels to joins us. "Can we pet them?"

Amy smiles. "Yes, of course, you can, but be gentle. Both of them are still recovering, and their skin is quite sensitive."

We sit on the cold, dirty floor as Amy opens the kennel. I don't immediately reach my hand out, but instead, talk to them as does Adriana. After a while, we feel confident and gently stroke Blaze. She closes her eyes and enjoys our touch. Ash's ears perk up, and almost like Blaze gives us her blessing, I bring my hand to Ash's belly and gently pet him. With his small puppy paw, he tries to play- fight with me, a move that makes Adriana's face light up. She has a beautiful smile, but it's often hiding behind her heartbreak.

We're interrupted as Jerry starts swearing.

"Fuck off, you pesky little shits!"

Jerry is running circles as a group of chicks follow him. I look at Adriana, and we both burst out laughing at the same time.

"Jerry, you finally got yourself a chick, shame it's of the feathered variety." Fred chuckles.

As Jerry continues to swear, even Hazel giggles at the sight of poor Jerry.

"Do you think someone will adopt them, Amy?" Adriana asks.

Amy kneels to join us. "Occasionally, we have genuine people come through here wanting to rescue a pet and provide a home for them. Other times, it's just a fad. The novelty of pet adoption wears off, and we often see them return."

"That's so sad," Adriana murmurs. "She's a mom trying to protect her baby."

"Just like you."

Fuck, did I just say that?

Adriana stops petting Ash. Her face falls, realization perhaps knocking sense into her. Moments later, her mouth curves upward as a small smile plays on her lips. "Just like me."

Much to my disappointment, Amy continues the tour of the shelter, and we leave Blaze and Ash alone. It's with great difficulty as I try to focus my attention on the other animals. Adriana seems to have the same problem, constantly looking behind her shoulder in the direction of Blaze's kennel.

"Are you thinking what I'm thinking?" I ask.

She beams when I say the words, both of us sneaking away from the group and heading back to the kennel. Once we're there, we sit on the ground, and without the kennel open, we are forced to poke our fingers through the metal grate to pet Blaze and Ash.

"She looks so helpless." Saddened by the sight in front of us, Adriana continues to stroke Blaze.

"She's a warrior. I can see it in her eyes. She's had a close call with death, seen her children suffer, but somehow she pulled through." I place the palm of my hand underneath her chin and caress her gently.

A lonely tear falls on Adriana's cheek. I'm uncertain what to do, wanting so much to wipe it away and help her overcome her pain, but I know it's not my place to interfere.

"You saved my niece," she mutters through her tears.

It was bound to come up. There's no escaping this topic.

"And you saved Charlie," she continues.

"I did what anyone else would've done in that situation." I continue to stare at Blaze and Ash. No matter what I do, where I go, I can't escape my actions, and it angers me. I want to escape to where it's impossible for anyone else to condemn me for my past.

There's only one place no one can find you.

Or one place where your sins may be forgotten, only to live eternally in the devil's paradise.

I pull myself off the ground and walk away without saying a word, abandoning Adriana once again.

Hazel is standing in an aviary feeding an injured bird. I owe her the courtesy of informing her I'm leaving. It's just all too much. She understands, but before I leave, she writes down her number and address in case I need her. I can see the pity in her eyes, and I feel ashamed for making her feel terrible for not being able to help me.

Leaning in, I hug her, and in return, she holds me tight before whispering the words I need to hear right at this moment, "My dear, you're lost, I see it in your eyes. Everyone finds their way home. You just need to find someone to guide you in the right direction."

I nod in understanding, now faced with the task of getting myself home. There's only one road out, and no better time to start walking it. Kicking dirt and stones, a rustle startles me, and Adriana is by my side.

"Why do you keep running from me?" she demands an answer, one I don't have.

Ignoring her question, I continue to walk, hoping she'll turn back around, but she pulls my arm back. Her eyes narrow, impatiently waiting for me to respond.

"What do you want me to say? Everyone says *you* saved Charlie. Thank God you were there! Well, I don't feel the same as everyone. I was doing something wrong. I shouldn't have been there," I shout, venting my frustration.

"And if you weren't there, she'd have been dead within minutes. My brother might as well have died along with her, their daughter would've been an orphan, and the rest of her family and friends would have been broken for life. How does that feel?" she yells.

I know how it feels. Chelsea's death impacted everyone who knew her. It even took the lives of her parents. It was the worst feeling, and no one should have to endure that.

"Exactly. You know the impact on those who survive. Whatever the fuck or whoever the fuck brought you there at that time was a godsend. Stop fighting what is." Her bold statement leaves me unable to speak.

I squat to the ground and run my hands through my hair, desperate for solitude, yet at the same time wanting to let go of this chain around my neck.

"Losing Chelsea was unbearable. I honestly thought Charlie would fix it. I was wrong."

"I know the pain all too well. I don't think there's a fix. That's the problem, right?" A sinister laugh escapes her mouth. "That's why we're all on the verge of being sent to the looney bin."

I pull her wrist toward me, alarming her. "This doesn't fix it, Adriana."

She pulls back forcefully, her heels walking away, escaping the conversation. I stand, my pace increasing to catch up with her. I pull her shoulder back, causing her to halt.

The anguish is overcoming her, the tears streaming down unwillingly. "Don't tell me this doesn't fix it. I'm so sick of feeling pain. How dare he leave me! How dare he leave our son!" she screams.

I let her get her words out, wanting to hold her tight, yet holding back, not wanting to confuse the moment.

"He didn't have a choice, Adriana," I whisper, pulling the sleeve on my jacket to wipe away her tears.

"He *did* have a choice. He refused treatment. My dad and Lex did everything they could to help him. In the end, he was selfish." Her chest is rising, the short breaths and panic sending her into an anxiety attack.

"Adriana..." I keep my voice low. "He was in his own pain. There's no way you'll ever be able to understand his intentions. You're here, Adriana. You have a son who loves and needs his mother. This..." I pull up her arm, the sun reflecting off her deep scars. "This isn't the answer."

She allows me to hold onto her arm while she catches her breath. "I didn't do it on purpose, at least not the first time. I was gardening, weeding Elijah's veggie patch when I tripped on my own feet and stumbled into the rose bush. It stung so much, yet at the same time, it took away the emotional pain I felt. The second time, I did it on purpose, that was the night I first attended the meeting."

I let go of her arm as we continue to stand on the side of the road.

"I'm sorry for your loss, Adriana. I only met him a few times, but from what I remember, he was a great guy."

Her smile remains fixed. "He was a great guy, the best friend and husband anyone could ask for."

A horn beeps in the distance, and the yellow bus is approaching us.

There's one more thing I want to say before the moment is lost. "Thank you, Adriana, for not judging me. But there's something I need to say..." I pause, forming the sentence in my head, not wanting to overwhelm her. "If ever you feel that way again, I'm just a phone call away. Please remember that."

She bumps her shoulder against my forearm with a wide grin. "And if ever you get all Charlie Sheen on us again, just flash your bat signal, and I'm there in a heartbeat."

I laugh painfully as the doors to the bus open. A sobbing Penny is sitting at the front with Hazel comforting her.

"What's wrong, Penny?" I ask worriedly.

"A cock pecked my ass!" she wails.

I turn to look at Adriana, attempting to keep a straight face.

Fred and Jerry have tears of laughter running down their eyes, and the bus driver barely contains himself, making it hard to control the laughter bubbling up inside of me.

"A cock pecked your ass? Poor Penny Tration," I tease.

Penny's sobs become fits of laughter. "Yeah, okay, I should be used to it."

We all fall into a fit of hysterics, and Hazel, as usual, is beaming with pride.

Laughter is the best medicine, they say, and so are a tranny's antics.

SEVENTEEN

It has been a week since I left the shelter wishing to escape reality, yet reality has come and found me.

It started on Tuesday. I was sitting at my desk in the office, the usual daily grind. It was ten o'clock when my boss called me to his office. He didn't sound unusual on the phone, so I thought nothing of it. That was until I walked into his office and saw Human Resource personnel sitting in there.

Economic downturn, blah blah blah, and I was handed my final paycheck.

There was no point arguing it as I returned to my desk to pack up my things. In the corner of my eye, I saw Nyree standing in the doorway. She told me three of her friends in the office were also let go. She was quite upset, but being in my own hell, it was pointless consoling her.

"So, how long do I have to keep standing here flashing some leg before you ask me out to dinner?" she asks teasingly.

My face spreads into a grin, and without looking into

her eyes, I continue to pack. "I was too distracted by the bust to notice the leg."

She threw a pen at me and burst into a fit of giggles.

"You look like you could use a home-cooked meal. How about my place next Friday night? I'm outta town this weekend."

An invitation to her place means one thing—she needs a good fuck and right now. I might be just the right person to give her what she needs.

Looking into her eyes, I see the lust and pleasure rolled into one. "Shall I bring dessert?"

Her eyes trace my body and make their way down to my cock. "That'll be great. No one wants to come empty-handed..."

The stir startles me. It's been a while and boy do I need to get fucking laid.

Losing my regular job feels so insignificant. I sit on a park bench thinking about my next move. Remembering the days of Harvard, there was so much drive, ambition, and aspiration in me to be a journalist. I reported on stories needing to be told, trying to change lives and make people see through my writing that we all need to reach out and help one another. We aren't all born with silver spoons in our mouths, and how the smallest act of humanity makes a difference.

Here, in California, I report stories about crime, celebrity fallouts, and other meaningless topics. This isn't who I want to be, and this is not satisfying my desire to be a better person.

As I walk back home, still no closer to what I want to do, I see a sign on my door.

I've been *evicted*.

The notice says all my belongings have been sent to a storage facility not too far from here. *Just fucking great.*

Officially, I'm now homeless.

I follow the directions to Hazel's home, surprised to find her house is, in fact, that farm I had stumbled upon that day I was lost. The serenity and peaceful surroundings ease the mounting pressure I feel over losing my apartment. It's a breath of fresh air, and I look above toward the clouds, thanking whoever blessed me with this amazing woman, a friendship, and support system I can't live without.

Hazel is sitting on the porch as I drive up the dirt road. It's small and quaint, surrounded by roses and carnations. She stands and greets me as I walk up the porch steps.

She calls my name and gently places her hands on my face. I feel her love, the motherly love I desperately missed from my mother. She takes me through her home. It's warm and inviting, filled with memorabilia of Richard and George. As we make our way back to the porch, she asks me to sit at the small table where she has fresh lemonade and homemade blueberry muffins. The view is amazing.

"I enjoy having company. Often when Miles is out of town, I head out to meet some old acquaintances for bridge night."

"Does Miles live here?"

I'm devouring these muffins, and they are practically melting in my mouth.

"Oh, no, dear. He has a home just around the corner.

It's such a beautiful home, and his daughter and grandson live with him."

"Is he out of town for work?"

"Mission work. Miles is a nurse. He volunteered down south when those awful tornadoes hit. He'll be back next week, and we'll be taking a vacation to the Netherlands," she adds.

"Netherlands?"

"Yes. My sister lives there, and I miss her dearly." Hazel talks with peace. She's content. How I yearn to be in her headspace right now.

"What do you do with the group when you're away?"

"Fred understands and chooses the time to vacation himself. Jerry... well, he sometimes takes a step back. I'm glad you took me up on my offer." She smiles.

"I feel weak asking for help."

"My dear boy..." she places her hand on mine, "... asking for help isn't a weakness, it's a strength. I have your room all ready for you."

She smiles, and I say no more.

Settling into Hazel's is exactly the kind of therapy I need. I don't allow her to spoil me, and often we work together in the kitchen preparing dinner. One night she asks me to prepare another two place settings, and before I know it, the doorbell rings.

The voice filters through the hall, and my heart skips a beat. Before I can fully register what's happening, Adriana pokes her head into the kitchen and greets me with a warm smile.

The tension which has built up releases when I see her.

It's stupid for me to jump to conclusions, assuming she'll hate me for my sordid past.

Her face looks different, a slight glow perhaps, a redness to her prominent cheeks. Although the dark circles still surround her eyes, there's a warm shade of brown illuminating her face. Wearing only a T-shirt which reads 'In Training For The Zombie Apocalypse,' her arms are no longer covered in raw cuts. Unfortunately, the scars still remain.

Penny's high-pitched holler enters the kitchen. She leans over and kisses Adriana on both cheeks and comes to my side, reaching out her hand, followed by a manly, "How's it going, pal?"

We burst out laughing at her feeble attempt to portray a man. Penny is all woman, despite the giant pecker sitting between her thighs.

The night is spent eating the meal we prepared, which, if I say so myself, turns out fantastic. After dinner, we settle for playing charades. It's one fail after another as Adriana and Penny team up against Hazel and me. Penny is the one who brought the game tonight, and after a few turns, we discover that it's adult charades. Surprisingly, Hazel isn't offended and enjoys the crude humor.

"Cat? Uh... butt? Oh my God, Penny, what the hell are you doing?" Adriana asks in frustration.

Penny is bending over doing something ridiculous, and not even I can figure it out.

"Um... kangaroo? I don't know," Adriana bellows.

The buzzer goes off.

"Doggy style!" Penny blurts out in annoyance.

"What? Really? Why the hell are you jumping like a kangaroo, then?"

"That isn't jumping! That's getting done from behind," Penny shouts.

Hazel and I are in stitches.

Penny clearly sucks at this game.

It goes on for a few more rounds before Hazel calls it a night. Penny gets a call from one of her friends, who she admits is a friend with benefits, and goes on to clarify that when she says benefits, she means he gives great head.

It's way too much information for me without any alcohol in my system.

Alone with Adriana, we move around quietly cleaning up. The seconds pass and feel like hours until we both try to break the silence at the same time.

"You first." I grin.

"I was going to ask how your week was, but I realized it probably sucked, you know, 'cause you're staying with Hazel."

"You know what? I'm really enjoying it here. It's giving me time to think about my next step," I respond at ease. With the room back to normal, we sit on the floor, picking at the leftover dessert. "How was your week?"

She lets out a sigh, followed by a hiccup. "I'm sorry. For some reason, ice cream does this to me."

"I think it's cute," I reassure her.

"Cute is bunnies and fluffy kittens. This is embarrassing." She hiccups again, and her face turns bright red.

We change the subject, moving our conversation onto Penny and how much she has in common with Eric.

"Just because they're both gay, we probably shouldn't assume they are a perfect match," I point out.

"Eric's taken, anyway," she says.

"Oh, I didn't realize he was seeing someone. Good for him."

She turns to look at me with a knowing grin. "Uh, really? Considering he's your nephew, I'd have thought you knew all the dirty secrets."

What did she just say?

"Excuse me? What does Tristan have to do with this?"

This time she places her hand on my arm. "Oh, Julian. You can't be that blind?"

"Maybe I am. Or maybe I've been too absorbed in my problems to see what was happening around me. I mean... I had an inkling at one point, but I thought the idea was ridiculous. He was fuck... I mean sleeping with a woman."

"Who would've thought, right? And look at how they came together because of you. It could be wedding bells before you know it."

Josie will fucking kill me, I think. Surely, she would know if her son is gay?

"Does it bother you?" she probes.

"No, not if it makes him happy. I miss him. Well, I miss hanging out with him. Sometimes it gets really lonely."

She nods, then withdraws. "The loneliness is palpable. Try being with couples all the time. It's like a hand constantly slapping you in the face. Don't get me wrong, I'm happy for them, it just reminds me of what I don't have."

"So, I guess you're referring to Charlie and Lex."

I glance aside. *Why did I bring this up?*

"Yeah... sorry. I can see it in your face. It hurts you to talk about them."

"No, Adriana... I just don't want to think about them anymore. Besides, one day you'll be in that place again. Look at Hazel."

Her eyes dart around the room, then focus on mine. "I don't want to. I want to remember him for the rest of my life. I'm scared someone else will erase my memories."

With a gentle smile, I wait for her full attention. "Adriana, impossible. No one can replace him or the memories."

Quick to change the subject, her face lights up, and she swiftly jumps to her feet. "I've got an idea. It's crazy and spontaneous, but it's just what we both need right now," she says excitedly.

It can't be sex. *Really, Julian? Why the fuck would you think that about her?* Don't be a shallow asshole.

I grin and say, "I'm all ears."

"I'll call you later with the details."

"Wait, you tell me we're about to do something crazy and spontaneous, then tell me you'll call me later with the details?"

She laughs, placing her hand on my arm reassuringly. "Okay, so perhaps spontaneous is the wrong word. I'll pick you up tomorrow morning."

"That's all? No clue?"

Adriana shakes her head, and despite my curiosity getting the better of me, it's nice to finally see her somewhat happy with a purpose.

"I promise, Julian, you'll have no regrets." She rests both her hands on my shoulders, her small stature only reaching my chin. "Do you trust me?"

I have every reason not to trust her.

Her bond to her brother can run deeper than I'm led to believe.

But what do I have to lose?

Absolutely *nothing*.

"I trust you... Adriana."

EIGHTEEN

"Are you sure you want to do this?"

"One hundred percent," I answer confidently. "Are you sure *you* want to do this?"

"One hundred and one percent." She smiles back.

Amy walks over and hands us paperwork which we both sign. I bend down to pet Blaze. She has a flicker of excitement in her eyes. Adriana holds onto Ash.

"Are you sure it won't traumatize them to be separated?" Adriana asks again.

"As long as they get enough attention and love, no," Amy reassures us.

It's exactly what we both need, and Hazel is beyond happy to have Blaze come live with us. I reassure her I'm looking for a place, but like always, she'll tell me to hush.

The ride back home is quiet as Blaze and Ash both rest their heads on Adriana's lap. It's not only the dogs who have a glimmer of hope in their eyes but Adriana as well. She's grinning from ear to ear, and undeniably, she is beautiful, scars and all.

"Andy is going to fall in love with Ash. I doubt very much I'll get him to bed at a reasonable hour tonight."

"He sounds like a typical kid."

"Yeah, he's a good kid. Just hyper, exactly the opposite of his dad." She sighs, glancing out the window.

We drive straight to the meeting, and as predicted, the group spends the hour playing with the dogs. Toward the end, Hazel politely asks us for our attention.

"Your weekly task," she announces as Jerry lets out a huge groan. "I want you to visit your happy place."

Penny is first to open her mouth. "Does Betty's Back Door Brothel count?"

"God, Penny, you're such a—" Jerry starts.

"Yada, yada, yada... talk to the hand 'cause the face ain't listening," Penny bites back.

Fred shakes his head, refusing to acknowledge a place of happiness, but as Hazel works her magic ways with him, he slowly comes around and mentions a hobby store with a motorized train in the front window he enjoys watching.

I, on the other hand, have nothing.

Every place I once enjoyed is tarnished with an unpleasant memory, all of which involve being high.

"You're struggling, I can see it," Adriana mentions, keeping her voice low from the others. "I feel the same."

"But you have Andy," I tell her, glancing sideways to catch a glimpse of her troubled face. "There must be some place which makes him happy and, in turn, makes you happy."

She remains quiet, lost in thought. Unusual from her normally vocal thought process. I place my hand on hers to reassure her.

"It'll come to us, somehow. In the meantime, do you

really think there's a place called Betty's Back Door Brothel?"

Adriana's shoulders begin to move up and down, her lips curving upward as laughter escapes her lips. With her mood lightening, she begins to bloom like a wilted rose basking in the sunshine.

She places her hand on my arm as I join in the private joke, laughing along with her, trying to control herself while the others turn to see us.

Penny, not knowing what's happening, joins in until the corner of Adriana's eye tears up, and she begs us to stop, or she'll pee her pants.

Hazel sits back, smiling proudly, "What do I always say?"

"Penny is *always* the best medicine," Adriana and I say in unison before falling into a fit of hysterics again.

I lay on my side as I stroke Blaze's fur. She closes her eyes, calm and appreciative of my gesture. In the quiet time, I hear the sound of an engine. Blaze can sense the presence as well, but her hearing is poor. There's a tap on the screen door, and I stand up to see who's there. I feel her before I see her, and Adriana's smiling back at me.

"Hey."

"Hey," she greets. "I've made some homemade treats for Blaze."

I open the door and let her in. She brushes past me, and this strange feeling hits me. I don't know what it is, but I know it's best to ignore it.

Adriana kneels to Blaze's level and strokes her belly.

"What, so no homemade snacks for me?" I tease.

"Here's the thing, I'm a terrible cook. I mean, I try to cook. It's okay, but it's not my forte."

"I don't believe you, Adriana. You say that about everything, and I can't point out one thing you do wrong."

"You're not looking hard enough," she says, and there it is, that self-doubt.

"I'm not looking for it."

Her pats slow down, and I see her body language change. "Elijah once said that he didn't care if I couldn't cook as long as I knew how to cook pot roast, that's all that mattered. He and my brother are pot roast freaks, and I blame my mom, who makes the meanest pot roast."

"Your mom sounds like a very nice woman."

"The greatest. I'd love for you to meet—" She stops mid-sentence

I don't want her to feel uncomfortable. "I would be honored to meet her as your friend." I place my hand on hers to reassure her, calm the guilt brewing inside of her. Almost instantly, I see her shoulders relax as she tilts her head slightly to stare back at me. Today they reflect a sign of hope, a woman trying her best to fight the odds of life.

"So, this happy place we're supposed to go to... how about I'll show you mine if you show me yours?" I offer.

She lets out a laugh. "Deal, you first..."

"You got a few hours?"

"I have two hours before I have to pick up Andy."

I stand up and reach out for her hand to pull her up. She follows me out the back door until we're standing on the porch.

"We're here."

"Uh... I don't get it?" she asks, confused.

"When I first came to LA, I stumbled on this place when I was lost one day. I can't explain it, there's something that draws me in. The horses, the greenery... it's so serene." I take a moment to appreciate the view. "I had no idea it belonged to Hazel, none whatsoever."

"Lost on the way to—"

I interrupt her with a slight annoyance. "No, if that's what you're asking."

"I... I wasn't really... I mean, I'm not saying it's wrong, just asking if that's—"

"Adriana, I said I wasn't."

She places her hand on my forearm, a friendly gesture but one I have become so accustomed to, easing my anxious nerves. "I'm sorry, Julian, diarrhea-mouth syndrome. I trust you're telling the truth."

"Does it bother you? Let's face it, we haven't talked too much more about it, and it's the giant elephant in the room."

"I know you loved Charlie. It's impossible not to. But I love my brother, and they are soul mates. Always were and will be. Redemption, Julian. You saved her."

"I did love her, Adriana, but she was a Band-Aid. And being in Hazel's group is teaching me that."

"Just like anyone who comes into my life will be a Band-Aid for Elijah," she mumbles.

I place my arm around her. "He was your husband, Andy's father. No one can replace him. All one can do is love you and Andy the way you deserve to be loved. In time, just don't push it away when you feel it."

"And what about you? Don't you think you deserve happiness?"

"Honestly? No. What am I, Adriana? I can't love without hurting those I love."

"You didn't hurt Chelsea."

"But if I had put my foot down, she'd still be here."

"Yeah, and if I weren't so caught up in my pregnancy,

maybe I might have noticed Elijah was sick and could've helped him," she answers back.

We both stay quiet, the enormity of our admissions deserving a moment of silence. There's a gentle breeze engulfing us, and the smell of lavender fills the air creating a calm between us.

"I'm scared of being alone, not now, but forever," I admit.

"You've got Blaze... and me. As long as we're friends, you're not alone," she says with ease.

"Does that mean you'll cook me pot roast when I'm suffering from male PMS?" I joke.

"Yeah, but I draw the line at picking up a pack of tampons for you."

"Great. Nice visual," I mock.

"Hey, you said it... man rags!"

"Too much. Eric... he's like the gay plague."

"Oh my, I'll tell him you said that."

"Don't you dare," I warn her.

She laughs, her gaze wandering toward the farm. All of her features soften, implying a calmness to her I've grown to love watching when she allows herself to be still and focus on her blessings.

"This place is so tranquil. The kind of place you could see yourself growing old in, don't you think?"

Fixated on the serenity, there's something to be said about the tranquility of being in a place, or presence, where the world stops revolving around you, and faith begins to restore. I never expected in my wildest of imagination to be sitting here, of all places, with Adriana Evans, clean and without cocaine running through my veins.

And while our words remain to ourselves, the silence between us is exactly what I need, and perhaps we both need. Our intent is to revive ourselves from our weakest of moments, lay the foundation to rebuild eternal happiness, just not in the way we have always envisioned and not with the people we assumed would be by our side for life.

"Yes, Adriana." I smile hopelessly at her, allowing the calm to wash over my sins and grant me the peace I deserve. "Exactly the place I see myself growing old in."

NINETEEN

L iving with Hazel is turning out to be very therapeutic.

It gives me a hell of a lot of time to think, spending countless hours in her garden with her animals, which Blaze seems to enjoy as well. I still apartment hunt, but everything I find says no pets, and there's no chance in hell I'm abandoning Blaze. Hazel scolds me as she rumbles through the discarded newspapers, quick to notice the red circles highlighting the vacancies. We had a long discussion one day, and I was very forthcoming with my intention to find my own way and not burden her. She explained that the process of finding oneself isn't something that happens overnight, plus she really enjoys my company. Something about the way I eat my cereal reminds her of her late son, George.

During the week, Adrianna brought Ash over to play with Blaze. It was quite the reunion, both dogs running around in the backyard like two of the happiest creatures I have seen. Blaze is healing well, according to Amy, and the fact that she can run is a huge improvement. I never felt so relieved when Amy informs me of Blaze's progress. Perhaps I don't hurt everyone around me.

It's a lazy Thursday afternoon spent sitting on the porch with my laptop, job hunting. I haven't heard about my manuscript which dampens my spirits.

I know the drill—countless resumes being sent in hopes of a bite and emails sent to a number of contacts, mainly interstate. I resist applying for any positions in New York, not yet, anyway. I may be on the road to recovery, but I'm not ready to head back to the place which started this whole clusterfuck.

My mind is occupied with a job listing for a newspaper located in a small town in Arizona when my cell beeps, startling my concentration.

Adriana: *My turn!*

A smile spreads across my face, welcoming the distraction. We exchanged numbers that day on the field trip, the whole 'if you need me, cry for help or give me a buzz' thing.

Me: *You're not taking me to a pedicure place or something? Girls and happy places = pampering and shopping.*

Adriana: *Oh damn, you ruined it! Henrietta my beautician would have been in heaven manicuring your man toes. I'll be at Hazel's to pick you up in an hour. See you soon. xx*

The one thing I have learned about Adriana is that she's punctual. If she tells you an hour, she means an hour.

Exactly an hour later, she's tooting her horn and yelling for me to hurry up.

Inside her car, I sit on the passenger side not recognizing the road we're on or have any sense of direction as to where we are going.

"Okay. Are you going to tell me where we are going now?" I beg, all whiney and very unmanly.

I really am not a surprise type of person. When I was thirteen, my mom and sister decided to throw me a surprise birthday party. I still remember the moment when I walked into the house, and everyone jumped out and yelled, "Surprise." I literally shit my pants. Embarrassing would be an understatement, mortifying would be more appropriate. No one knew it happened. I just ran up to the bathroom and locked the door shut until everyone left.

"You're terrible. Not much longer, okay? Don't worry, I'm not taking you to a secluded part of the woods so I can murder you with an ax." She rolls her eyes at me in amusement.

"Huh... so explain the ax in the trunk?"

"You never know when you may need to chop wood... for a fire," she adds with a devilish grin.

"We live in California. It's like a hundred degrees out here. Should I dial 9-1-1 now or give you a head start?"

"Okay, we're here," she cheers.

I look out the window and see a sign which says 'Farmer Joe's Apple Picking Farm' in bright colors. We get out of the car, and in a closer view, I see rows and rows of apple trees without an end in sight. It almost looks like a maze.

"This here is my happy place. Was *our* happy place," she quickly corrects herself. "Before Elijah passed, we discovered this place on the way to the beach. It was supposed to be a pit stop to pick up a few apples, but we got lost in here for hours. Picking out apples and talking about anything and everything."

Her face radiates as she talks openly about her husband, and I listen eagerly, enjoying this side of Adriana she rarely shows.

"There are so many things I didn't know about him, the smallest things from his childhood."

"It's beautiful, Adriana, and I happen to have a thing for apples."

She hands me a basket. "Well, then, what are we waiting for?"

In my entire life, I never thought apple picking would be this satisfying, searching apple after apple for the perfect one. Some are small, some are large, some are bruised, and some are oddly shaped. *Is there a perfect apple?* Who knows. All I know is that I'm looking for the perfect one, a delicious, perfectly shaped ruby red apple that will make my mouth water.

We talk a lot about life, mainly Andy. Adriana is happily chatting, and I'm eagerly listening. When the subject changes, we start talking about my childhood, and I find myself opening up about Chelsea.

"I hated the way Chelsea would always talk about kissing. I must have been in sixth grade, and all she'd talk about was kissing. I may have thought it was the grossest thing in the world. She even told me how she practiced on her pillow." I cringe, recalling the memory like it was yesterday.

"Oh, we all did that. It's like a rite of passage into puberty. I'd kiss my pillow and actually hold it like a face." She blushes, quick to cover it with a laugh.

"You didn't..." I tease.

"Sure did. Occasionally, I'd grope the pillow's butt, but hey, let's not go there." She giggles.

I shake my head at her confession. "Who would you picture kissing?"

"Let's see... around that time was my *Saved by the Bell* phase, and I had a huge crush on Slater," she admits.

"As in Mario Lopez?"

Her eyebrow perks before she blurts out unexpectedly, "Should I be worried you knew that?"

"No... I had a huge crush on Jessie," I admit.

"Please... I bet you it was only because of that stripper movie. God, my brother would practically watch that movie every night on mute."

"My turn to be disturbed. Sure... it was a great movie. Really educational," I lie pathetically.

"Educational, my butt. Oh, look at this apple... it kinda looks like a butt!" She laughs really hard, and I can't help but mimic her actions. It could've been a clone of J.Lo's butt, it's that exact.

The laughter dies down as the conversation switches to a more serious topic.

"If Chelsea were here today, do you think you would've stayed together?" she asks.

The question catches me off guard. It's something I've never thought about until now.

"Knowing Chelsea, she'd have married a jock. She was too into being popular."

"That's normal at that age."

"Maybe..."

"Charlie mentioned you the other day," she blurts out.

I shift my head down. *Am I supposed to answer that?* My silence isn't helping, but I haven't thought about Charlie in a while.

"I don't know how to respond to that," I say, lowering my voice.

"Well, what's the first reaction you had in your head?"

"To ignore you. That I shouldn't talk about her. I don't want to talk about her. That I hadn't thought about her for a while."

Adriana purses her lips. "She's incredibly grateful for what you did. After all, if it weren't for you, she wouldn't be living and breathing... neither would her daughter, Ava."

I remain quiet, unsure about how to respond.

"And she hopes you're recovering."

"Did you—"

"No," Adriana interrupts. "My therapy, Hazel, and our group, I keep to myself. I like to keep things private and away from everyone who knew Elijah."

I nod, understanding her need to keep things to herself given her family and friends are known to be intrusive.

"If Charlie could reach out to you, I know she would. But my brother is—"

"I'm not here to cause a rift between them, okay?" I run my hands through my hair, trying to make sense of my thoughts. "It's just..."

"You're scared?"

"Not scared. It's just that, for once I feel like I'm moving forward with life. I'm breaking down all my walls. I've actually got a date with someone tonight."

"A *date*?" The pitch of her tone is high, and I see her attempt to pull an apple from its stem impatiently. Her body language changes as her shoulders tense.

Quick to brush it off, I reply, "Someone I used to work with. It's just dinner."

"Dinner leads to sex, Julian. You're a male, after all," she says plainly.

"That's a very stereotypical comment," I tell her, slightly offended. "It's not all about sex."

Despite what people think, it really isn't. I'm at a point in my life when I know the difference. Sometimes I need a good fuck, and other times I crave companionship. They don't always mix together, and it's for that exact reason why I have to set boundaries and not fall for the obvious.

She lets out a huff, scrambling her apples around. "It always is. Why would a single man your age want anything but sex with a new girlfriend?"

"Don't put me in that category, Adriana. I'm not after a heavy relationship, but I'm not exactly willing to throw myself into a relationship based on sex only, which I have done on more than one occasion. It never ends well," I openly admit, annoyed at her assumption of me. "I've got a hell of a lot of soul-searching to do. I've only had two serious relationships, a girl in college and Charlie. Look where that went."

"I wasn't born yesterday, Julian. Women throw themselves at you. This chick would be expecting nothing less." The malice in her tone catches me off guard, offending me with her comment.

"So, are you trying to say I'm worth nothing but a good time in the bedroom?" I ask hastily.

She stumbles on her words. "No... I don't mean that. Quite the opposite. I'm not relaying my message properly."

"What message is that?"

"Despite what you may want, women do see you as a drop-dead gorgeous man who they envision in their bedroom. I know you're trying to find yourself, and I'm sorry for making you feel worthless. I've only ever had one relationship... and if God weren't so fucking selfish, he'd still be the one." She stands and dusts off her pants.

My immediate thought shifts to Adriana, forgetting about our argument. "Hey, you okay?"

She stops, her eyes slightly glazed over. "No... it sucks. What the hell do I know about dating? I know I'll probably have to do it one day even though the thought of it makes me want to break out in hives and vomit profusely."

"A date?" I question.

"Yes. And have sex with someone else. I'm not a nun."

"You'd be a waste of a nun," I point out, softening my tone.

"That's a shitty pick-up line, Baker." She punches my arm softly, followed by a relaxed laugh.

I nod in agreement. "Never said I was a pro, don't be fooled by the exterior."

We spend another hour walking through the fields, lost in mindless chatter. As the sun slowly sets, we call it a day and drive back home.

Adriana pulls the car up in front of Hazel's home, prompting me to unbuckle my belt.

"Thank you for today, Adriana. I've got enough apples to feed a herd," I joke.

She continues to stare out the window, lost in thought. I give her a moment. Adriana needs time to process her thoughts, and pushing her doesn't get you anywhere but into a heated debate.

"No, thank you, Julian. Being able to talk openly about Elijah means a lot to me, and I can't believe how much I miss talking about him."

"I wish you could see your face when you talk about him. You look so alive," I admit.

"My family walks on eggshells whenever his name is brought up. It's like they think I'll break down, so they just avoid talking about him. I hate they do that."

I place my hand on hers reassuringly. "Adriana, you need to tell them it's okay to talk about him, in fact, it's therapeutic. Sometimes you're going to have bad days and get emotional, and that's okay, too."

"You're right. I need to stop being treated like a porcelain doll. When a porcelain doll breaks, what do you do? You glue her face back together with superglue," she rambles.

My shoulder moves involuntarily as the laughter consumes me. "I wouldn't know, Adriana, I've never owned one and don't plan to anytime soon."

A smile traces her lips before she boots me out and wishes me well on my date.

TWENTY

I sit across the table from Nyree.

The date is nothing out of the ordinary so far. She's a fantastic cook, preparing some Spanish meal which I have no chance of pronouncing. Most of the time we talk about work since it seems to be the only thing we have in common.

The apartment is opposite Long Beach with a view of the ocean, the air lingering of salt and humidity. With the balcony doors open, there's a soft breeze blowing against the sheer purple organza curtains which hang by the door.

"It's a nice place you have," I say politely.

It's an open-plan living and dining room combined. The furniture is all white but doesn't appear too sterile. It's nicely decorated with splashes of bright colors and a million cushions.

What's with the cushions? I'm not a picky guy, but I think cushion-loving women need to come with a warning.

"I love this place. Moved here about two years ago." She finishes the last drop of wine, informing me she's going to grab some more and to make myself comfortable on the couch. I never really understood when people say to make yourself comfortable. Isn't that what you would naturally do? Why would you purposely make yourself uncomfortable?

As I move over, I sit on the edge, not sure if I'm allowed to mess the carefully aligned cushion thing going on. Grabbing my cell, I text a message just out of curiosity, wondering if this needs to be brought up in our therapy sessions.

> **Me:** *Since you're a woman, can you please explain the purpose to me of why you need a million cushions on a couch?*

I'm not expecting an immediate response, knowing Adriana has a work function going on. Moments later, I'm surprised to see my screen light up.

> **Adriana:** *I'm guessing date night is getting cozy. To be honest, I hate cushions. You only need one. Are you expected to take them on and off every day?*

The comment throws me off. It isn't at all like that. *I don't want that, do I?* Nyree is gorgeous, sexy, but something about tonight feels off.

> **Me:** *She's gone to get more wine, so to answer your question, it's not one of those dates. You know Eric is a serial cushion freak.*

Nyree is taking a long time to get wine. I poke my head to the side, unable to see her shadow in the kitchen. Maybe she stores wine somewhere else in her apartment. Like where... her bedroom? I enjoy the solitude, taking advantage of texting while she's gone.

> **Adriana:** *Eric is a freak in everything. More wine eh? That can't be a good sign. Losing your touch, Baker?*

This feeling creeps in, a part of me telling me to leave now. Why, though? Adriana doesn't say anything untrue. Typing at record speed, I send a text followed by regret. I shouldn't have said that, I don't know what it means, and the worst part is, I don't want her to feel guilty.

> **Me:** *Maybe, or maybe it's just the wrong person.*

I hear the gentle footsteps behind me and feel the touch of Nyree's hands massaging my shoulders. I close my eyes for a few moments, hoping her touch connects with me somehow, but it might as well be a ninety-year-old woman touching me because it feels wrong. All wrong.

I shouldn't have sent that text.

Why did I say that?

She doesn't respond. I hurt her. I made her feel guilty, and I know it.

I crossed the line in our friendship, and the thought alone is tearing me up inside.

Nyree must be sensing the tension in my muscles, so she squeezes harder, then moves toward the sofa. She's wearing a thin black negligee. It's very sheer, her pink nipples erect under the garment. Between her long, tanned legs and perfect breasts, she is absolutely stunning and irresistible to any man before her.

Except me.

Watching this model-like woman stand in front of me, ready to pleasure me in a way I haven't been pleasured in a long time, one would think my pants would be ready to burst. Yet, I sit here, flaccid as a starfish, and all I can think about is how smooth her skin is.

When all I want to kiss are scars.

How her eyes shine brightly, full of life.

When all I want to look into are the eyes of a warrior.

How her lips are plump and luscious red.

When all I want to taste are red, raw, chapped lips.

Nyree reaches out to touch me, and I recoil instantly, startled by my reaction. I can't feel this way about Adriana. You're her friend and have formed a special bond with her which can't be broken. These thoughts are poisonous like a sick carousel of emotions. *Do not break that trust.*

"Is something the matter?" Nyree appears taken aback.

"I, uh... I've got a lot on my mind," I respond.

She pulls back, the hurt evident on her face. "A lot on your mind or someone else on your mind?"

I give her my full attention, and I know taking the next step will be wrong. I will *maybe* satisfy myself sexually, but for once, I know the consequences and don't need another Band-Aid to fix the problem temporarily.

"I need to go. I'm sorry, Nyree."

She covers herself with a cushion. *Ha! So that's what they are used for.*

"Is she worth it?" she asks.

I think about my answer. "She's worth it. She just belongs to someone else. Always will."

∽

It's two in the morning, and I'm wide awake. Tonight didn't go how I planned, and throwing fuel into the fire, my feelings surface, and now it's all I can think about. Whichever way I turn, I'm torn. The selfish side of me refuses to ignore the feelings extending more than just friendship. Yet across the pond, inside my restless brain, the rational side of me is begging for my thoughts to clear and understand the magnitude of desiring someone unattainable.

There's unattainable, and then there's Adriana.

The next day, I still haven't heard from her. I chose to remain quiet, busying myself with some freelance work I managed to pick up. It isn't the greatest of income, but my bank account looks the healthiest it has in a long time.

As the afternoon rolls around, Hazel suggests we feed the animals, something I find very therapeutic. We talk a lot about life, her husband, and son. Hazel is fascinated with my time abroad, wanting to know more about my life before coming here. The more I speak, the more I realize how much my life has changed. The old Julian had no hesitation jumping on a plane, traveling to remote areas of the world desperate for a journalistic insight into third-world poverty. On reflection, I'd barely stayed in one location for any length of time until I reached New York. The stability of a full-time position plus freelance work for the *New York Times* brought on more problems than I ever cared to admit.

The second I stopped moving, all my addictions began.

"I'm scared, Hazel," I say while patting Cletus, Hazel's California Vaquero, known to be the wild horse on the farm. "This is the longest time since my time in New York, I have been stationed in one spot."

"Is this where you see yourself settling one day?"

"No, LA was an escape. From the moment I left college, all I wanted to do was travel. And I did, I loved every minute of it, but then I almost talked myself into leaving that life behind."

"Wanderlust." She smiles, placing her hand on my arm. "It's embedded in you."

"How do I know? What if it's not embedded but a coping mechanism?"

"My dear, I think deep inside the emotional drive behind your travels far outweighs your doubt. You've helped people all over the world. You've raised attention to villages with no fresh water, children being born into slavery. Your heart is purer than you care to admit, and right now, much like Cletus, something has spooked you."

I turn to face Hazel, half expecting to see a crystal ball in her hand. She sees things people have not seen yet for themselves.

"It's getting late," I tell her, letting out a long-winded sigh. "How about I cook dinner tonight?"

She laces her arm into mine as we begin to walk back. "I'd love that."

Feeding off our earlier conversation regarding my time abroad, I make a dish I enjoyed in Tanzania—pilau. Hazel devoured the meal, praising me on my cooking skills. With the remains, she places it in a container and announces she's heading to Miles' house knowing he'll enjoy the meal too.

Alone, with my thoughts and still no response, I decide to make good and not allow the silence between us to create any animosity or unwanted attention.

Me: *I've been thinking about you and dating. I feel bad that you probably suck at it so I'm taking you on a date tomorrow but it's not an official date. More like a date practice run with no happy ending—yes, I had to go there. Show me what you got.*

I throw my cell on my pillow, hoping she'll respond and welcome the idea but notice the time is after midnight. The topic of 'dating' is obviously a sore point for Adriana with a valid reason attached. She made it clear—Elijah has been her first everything. And with that said, her fear is with merit.

Against my pillow, the cell lights up.

Adriana: *Thanks for telling me I suck, which I do. I have absolutely no comment on your happy ending comment which is odd since I always have a come-back on everything, right? Ok, you're on Baker. I'll wear my date outfit, or shall I call it slutty black dress and I'll even shave my legs!*

I can't contain the smile on my face, glad she isn't offended by my text.

Me: *Why on earth are you awake? Should I shave my legs too? I actually did shave my legs... well, more like trimmed them. Years of playing basketball. Eric has on more than one occasion complimented my trimming skills.*

Adriana: *Yeah ok, go for it again. But don't tell me what else you're gonna shave cause that's TMI. Insomnia's a bitch.*

We agree to meet at a little French restaurant tomorrow night at seven. Adriana says she'll see if she can get a sitter, but then says Eric owes her a favor for using all her hairspray the last time he was over.

I don't ask any questions. Eric's hair needs a damn committee to run it.

I still don't know if I'm doing the right thing. I am trying my best to follow my instincts, and the thing which worries me the most—it always leads to *her*.

TWENTY-ONE

The waiter leads us to a secluded part of the restaurant.

In a polite gesture, I pull Adriana's chair out, ignoring her skin glistening under the dim lighting in this gorgeous black dress she's wearing. With her hair in soft curls and a touch of makeup enhancing her already perfect features, she looks absolutely breathtaking.

She thanks me for the kind gesture until we both fall into an awkward silence. I have no clue why this feels hard, and then suddenly, my gaze meets her, and we both laugh.

"This is weird," she admits.

"I'm not sure if I should be offended, and you're supposed to be pretending this is a real date. Now, start flirting with me or something," I joke.

"Oh, I got it! I'm new in town, can you give me directions to your apartment?" She attempts to pull a straight face.

I almost spit out my wine at the cheesy pick-up line. "Keep going."

"Your breasts remind me of Mount Rushmore, my face should be among them," she continues.

I let out a huge roar, almost on the verge of tears. She can't keep a straight face, and I love watching her so carefree and relaxed.

"I'm concerned about the size of my breasts now," I say between laughs.

"Wait, one more.... I've saved the best for last. Drum roll, please..."

Tapping my hands against the table, I make a drumming sound.

"You're just like my little toe because I'm going to bang you on every piece of furniture in my home."

This time she's unable to contain herself.

"Adriana, where on earth? No, wait... I think I know from who."

"Oh, those were the G-rated ones. Trust me, I've heard crude in its finest form. Eric has the mouth of a sailor, although I think I'm immune to his dirty humor now."

The waiter returns and takes our order. He leaves in a flash, allowing us more time to talk.

"Do you even know what you ordered?" she asks.

"Yes. I understand French, somewhat."

"So, did I order something weird?"

"A gentleman never tells," I tease.

"It's brains, isn't it? It is just like that episode when Donna says it is mushy, and Brenda tells her it is brains," she complains.

"When she thought she ordered the veal?"

She raises an inquiring eyebrow. "Uh, yeah... okay, your 90210 knowledge may be a red flag at this part of the date."

I grin, raising the wine glass to my lips. "Kelly Taylor.

Biggest. Crush. Ever. Actually, I still have a thing for Jennie Garth."

"A blonde. Interesting," she says in a quieter tone.

I think about her comment. "Interesting because..."

"Because you seem to like a particular type of girl, you know, brown hair, tanned skinned, stunning," she rambles on.

"That's judging me, isn't it? I don't have a type. In fact, you—" I cut myself off, immediately not believing I almost said the words that will change our relationship.

There's no relationship, and we're just *friends*.

There can't be a relationship.

Be careful of the words that come out of your mouth. Adriana isn't like everyone else.

"What were you going to say to me?" She swallows, nervously toying with the napkin in her lap.

"Uh, no... I was..." *Quick, think of something!*

"Please... just be honest with me," she begs.

I stare into her green eyes, searching for a piece of her that will give me the courage to say what I want to say, what has been eating me inside and tearing me to pieces. I see something, but that can easily be my overactive imagination. I'm terrified of hurting her. She doesn't need the burden in her life.

"Adriana, I can't admit to you my feelings because it isn't fair to you."

"Shouldn't I be the one to decide that?"

"I think you're beautiful..." I hush, unable to continue looking at her. My palms are sweaty, and I play with the edge of the tablecloth. Looking into her eyes is too intimate, and that level of intimacy is something I know Adriana is uncomfortable with.

"I don't feel that way."

My face meets hers, and I see the turmoil she's in. "Why?"

"Because I'm broken. I feel like a vase in a store that's been chipped and cracked and left on the sale rack on clearance at ninety-nine cents, and everyone ignores it because they can't repair it."

"Maybe it doesn't need to be repaired. Maybe it needs to be accepted for its imperfect perfections."

Her eyes are clouded, lips quivering. I don't want her to cry. It pains me to see how much she devalues her own worth.

The food arrives, distracting us from the intense conversation. She moves the food around her plate, a loss of appetite after the realizations of tonight weighs on her mind.

"Adriana, let's put that conversation aside. I want you to enjoy tonight. No date stuff... just as friends, okay?"

The switch in topics seems to brighten her mood. "So, I picked up Andy today from day-care, and he was walking around with handbags."

I laugh. "Too much influence from Eric?"

"His cousin, Amelia, is the complete opposite. She wears superhero costumes every day and literally repels anything girly."

"I thought it was odd until Charlie explained the reason why."

I see Adriana's shoulders tense. "I'm surprised Lex allowed you to speak to her."

Unsure of how to respond to that, I take a bite of my food, ignoring Adriana's shift in mood which is of no surprise anymore.

"I'm sorry. I guess you wouldn't want to hear his name. After all, he stole your girl, right?" Her smile fades.

"She wasn't mine to begin with."

The chime of my cell interrupts us. I see the familiar number and ask to be excused while I take the call—it's Mr. Grimmer.

I step outside the restaurant and stand by the door as I answer the call. At first, Mr. Grimmer starts talking about my manuscript and his review. He goes on and on about certain chapters, people, about how I captured this and how, at certain moments, his emotions got the better of him, and he wasn't sure if he could continue. It feels like hours of standing here, not surprised one bit when Adriana comes outside to check on me.

She seems to have understood that the call was important enough to warrant walking away, but I reach out and hold onto her arm and mouth for her to stay.

"Son, you've got yourself a publishing deal. Welcome to Lantern Publishing Group," Mr. Grimmer announces.

The shock stills me.

Did I hear right?

I actually accomplished a dream.

The enormity of the situation leaves me breathless. "Are you serious? I can't... wow... thank you so much."

Mr. Grimmer asks to meet me in his office first thing tomorrow morning to go over the publishing contract.

I did it!

I hang up the cell, Adriana now waiting impatiently for me to say something.

"C'mon, whatever it is that made you smile like that must be good. What happened? The suspense is killing me."

"I got the publishing deal," I say, shocked by the outcome. "My manuscript is going to be published."

Somewhere in her congratulations, I have a moment of

clarity. It's all coming together, life has a purpose again, and most importantly, I can't think of anyone else I want to share this moment with.

The overwhelming feeling consumes me, and without thinking, I pull Adriana's face toward me, pressing my lips against hers. The taste of her lips feels so right like I have been waiting a lifetime to feel this kind of moment, but it only lasts a few seconds before she pushes my chest away, breaking me from this moment.

Her eyes are laced with guilt, wiping her lips with the back of her hand.

"I'm s-sorry," I stutter, immediately regretting my actions.

A lonely tear escapes her eye, and as I reach out to touch it, she turns her back and runs away into the night.

Leaving me to once again to bask in my mistakes.

TWENTY-TWO

I haven't spoken to Adriana since the night at the restaurant.

It's been five days to be exact.

My time has been occupied with Mr. Grimmer and working through edits of my manuscript. Although I've been busy with work, the guilt of my actions weighs heavily on my mind. I pushed Adriana too far when I knew she was already standing on the edge. She reached out to me wanting a friendship, and I took it in the wrong direction. My stupid feelings got in the way. Again. Desperately wanting to call her to apologize, I think about my past and what I'd normally do in this situation.

I'd have chased the girl.

But this girl is different.

I can't chase someone who isn't even in the running.

She belongs to someone else—that will never change. And I love her even more for that reason. Why? I have no idea.

You said you love her, jackass. *Remember, you aren't supposed to fall in love so easily?*

No, I'm not, and I don't even know what love is. I told Chelsea I loved her, and how naïve was I to confuse lust and love.

And then there was Charlie. I did love her, I can't deny that, but now I believe love comes in many forms, and sometimes, it's powerful enough to be your reason for breathing. Charlie, as much as I did love her, was never my reason for breathing. She was my life jacket, keeping me alive in a blustering storm.

Late in the afternoon, I sit in my favorite spot on the porch stroking Blaze's fur. My cell begins ringing, startling a few blue jays sitting on the porch ledge.

"Son, I have some exciting news for you," Mr. Grimmer greets me without a hello, the positive vibe piquing my curiosity.

"I could use some exciting news right now," I confess.

"I know, I can sense that," he says, without judgment in his tone. "Lantern Publishing has a sister company, and they are mighty impressed with your work. They want you to fly over and do signings across the country, including a book reveal party."

The excitement floods my veins, the familiar rush from my hard work paying off. I've had many moments like this, such as when I graduated from Harvard with honors to the first time I'd published an article in the *New York Times*. Memorable moments which have been lost in my own insecurity over the last few years.

"I'm grateful to be given this opportunity. For how long and where?"

"At least six months, and... it's Sydney, Australia," he reveals.

My brain takes a moment to register six whole months on the other side of the world. Visiting Australia has always been on my bucket list. I have absolutely no doubt I'll enjoy such a beautiful country.

"It'll be all expenses paid. I'll be honest with you, son, I haven't seen an offer extended to an author this generous in quite some time. You should be proud of yourself."

"I am... it's huge and such a great opportunity." The excitement slowly starts to build again. "When will I leave?"

"Sunday night."

"As in five nights from now?"

"Yes. They want this on the shelves by Christmas. Time to start packing your bags. This will be the beginning of an extremely rewarding career." He continues to congratulate me and speaks briefly about the finer details.

Financially, I'm back in the game and able to get ahead again. It's a golden opportunity, yet I am unable to fully appreciate it as the thought of being away makes my heart beat abnormally. This is ridiculous, a dream come fucking true, and I don't want to leave someone who one... could never have feelings for me the way I want them to, and two... is just a friend.

I hear a rustling noise beside me. Hazel sits down with Blaze in the middle of us.

"I didn't mean to eavesdrop."

"Hazel, this is your home. I can't thank you enough for opening it up to me."

She gives me a few moments. "I've been given the opportunity of a lifetime, Hazel. Why am I not jumping over the moon?"

"Because your heart wants what it wants." She smiles.

"My heart has been very wrong in the past. Why should I believe it now?"

"Julian, you have to accept that people, events... they

happen for a reason. These people who came into your life... don't question your love for them. Be grateful and treasure the experience."

"I have to go to Sydney... I know it's the right thing to do."

"Then go. Follow what's inside here." She points to my heart. "It's never wrong when you're listening with all honesty."

"The problem is, I think someone is clouding my judgment." It's the first time I have admitted my feelings to anyone, besides, of course, Adriana. I've been bottling it up waiting to see if it will magically disappear. Turns out, it only intensifies. "I don't even know where to begin with it. I just know it hurts to think I won't see her face whenever I want."

"She's alive, living, and breathing? She walks this earth?"

"Yes."

I don't know where Hazel is going with this.

"Then distance is only a minor obstacle. My point is, you can see her whenever you want, and you can talk to her whenever you want. Technology these days is remarkable. If only they had Skype in heaven." She smiles fondly.

I place my arm around her shoulders, thanking her for everything. Hazel will always be the calm throughout the storm, the reason when hope fails. A mother, a friend—a confidant.

"What about Blaze?" I ask in concern. I haven't even thought about her.

"She'll stay where she belongs, right here. I wouldn't have it any other way."

And so, it's settled. I'm moving to Australia for six months.

There's a lot to do in five days, and to top that off, Hazel suggests that instead of having our normal meeting, we have a gathering here at her place as a farewell. I thank her for not surprising me since I hate surprises, and she knows exactly that.

Saturday night rolls around fast. Time is ticking. The house is decorated with streamers and balloons by the decorating committee consisting of the one and only Penny.

"Is it just my imagination or are all the balloons shaped like a—"

Penny cuts me off. "You're a dirty boy, and I think you need to drown yourself in a slippery otter."

"Slippery otter?"

"Puu... ss... yy," she annunciates.

I shake my head while smirking and make my way to the door to answer the knocking.

"Hello, I'm homo!" announces Eric.

Tristan follows him, rolling his eyes at Eric's antics, and now that I'm aware of his sexuality, I search for something different. There's nothing but the same old Tristan in front of me. I reach out and pull him into a hug. I'm sure going to miss the kid.

"You're choking me," he coughs before lifting his gaze to see Penny. "And is that a man?"

I let go of him. "Eric, Tristan, meet my good friend, Penny."

"Penny... Penny Tration," she adds.

Eric roars in laughter, but Tristan is a little more reserved.

"Oh, honey, I love it!" Eric gasps.

Penny pulls Eric and Tristan by their arms to the back, chatting away. I only hear the words, "Oh, you, twinks, you're adorable together. Who does your hair, darling?"

The doorbell rings again, and it's Fred and Jerry.

Fred is carrying a plate of Jell-O. Hazel thanks him and ushers him to the kitchen. Jerry looks different. His hair is cut short, and I think it's brushed.

"Looking good, Jerry. I don't swing that way, but it's nice to know you care," I joke.

"Ha-ha. Penny took me to some salon where the drags did a number on me. I got a date tonight with a girl from my local comic bookstore," he grunts.

"A girl who works at a comic bookstore? Damn, now that's a catch."

"Yeah, she's into a lot of the retro comics like me," he says, shrugging his shoulders.

"I'm proud of you." I pat his back. "Just be yourself and have fun, okay?"

He nods, making his way to the snack table where he shoves all the Cheetos into his mouth—poor comic book girl.

I head outside to the porch to mingle. I'm a little nervous and don't ask Hazel about Adriana. Everyone here deserves my attention, and despite the tight chest from my mistakes being greater than I ever imagined, I manage to put on a grateful smile for everyone.

"You're gonna love Sydney," Tristan says to me, stepping away from Penny and Eric.

"I'm sure I will," I agree, taking a sip of my beer. "Hey, kid, what was the real reason you left?"

Tristan shuffles his feet, his shoulders slumping as he becomes agitated by the question. "Mom's husband, John, had a problem with me..." He gazes at Eric, and like there's some sort of connection, Tristan finds his voice. "He beat me because he found out I was gay."

My heart drops as he confirms my suspicions. Roy is a fucking asshole for touching the poor kid.

"I should've helped you, saved you from him," I bellow, shaking my head with anger. "I was too messed up to see others around me hurting."

"You did, you gave me a place to stay. You introduced me to new friends who helped me find my way. You did more than you can ever imagine."

"Oh, kid, you're gonna make me cry."

"Man hug?" he jokes.

I pull him into me and hug him tightly, crimpling his hair.

"Not the hair!" he complains.

I notice Blaze's ears perk up, and she runs off toward the side of the house. Seconds later, we see Ash bolt through the lawn with a happy Blaze following him.

It can only mean one thing—*she's here*.

Staring down at the dirt, I try to regain the courage to look her in the face and push away any unlawful feelings I have toward her. She turns the corner, but before her, I see a little boy running across the lawn chasing the dogs.

It's her son, no doubt. He's very small and looks nothing like Adriana. If I remember correctly from the times I met Elijah, he's the spitting image of him. Now I understand why it's so hard for Adriana to move on when she has a son who'll forever remind her of the man she loves.

"Eric!" Andy yells. "Mama let me bring Ash!"

Eric runs over and pulls Andy into an embrace, burying his head into his hair much to Andy's annoyance.

A moment later, Adriana appears, wearing cut-off denim shorts, white Adidas sneakers, and a T-shirt which reads 'Keep Calm and Call Batman' with a bat logo beneath it. My heartbeat, which has momentarily stopped the moment I laid eyes on her, begins to drum inside my chest the closer she walks toward us. Her presence is powerful and magnetic with its force, and is exactly what has been missing today, or perhaps, for my entire life.

Standing on the porch, she quickly introduces Andy.

"Oh, darling, he's gorgeous. How did you pop that boy out of your tiny vag... frame of yours?" Penny corrects herself.

"He was cesarean, so all intact, Penny." She winks as Penny raises her hand to applaud her with a high-five.

It's refreshing to see her relax, but she has yet to come my way. The moment she does, I'm a bunch of nerves, and she knows me well enough to sense how uncomfortable I am.

I did ruin things. *Again.*

"Andy, come here for Mama, please." He lets go of Eric's hand and runs toward Adriana. "Andy, this is my good friend, Julian," she introduces me, her eyes meeting mine with a genuine smile.

Andy squints his eyes, staring at my face.

"Mama, he looks like Bruce Wayne," he says, tugging on her sleeve.

"He does." She laughs, keeping her gaze fixated on mine, and in hers, I see forgiveness.

I kneel to his level. "Hey, buddy, nice to meet you."

"Are you Blaze's daddy?" he asks.

"I guess you could say that," I reply.

"I don't have a daddy. My daddy has to work in heaven forever."

My heart is torn when he says the words, and I see Adriana's face fall instantly.

"I'm sure you've got plenty of people who love you just like your daddy. Do you want to get some treats for Blaze and Ash?"

He nods his head in excitement, his momentary admission overcome by feeding the dogs.

Hazel comes over and smothers him with her kisses, and he's off again.

I turn to Adriana, willing my apology to be said. "Adriana—"

"I shouldn't have run off. I'm sorry," she interrupts.

"No, you had every right to run off. I should've considered how it would affect you. I was caught up in the excitement, and it was selfish of me. I don't want to lose our friendship."

"Neither do I..." she trails off, rocking back and forth with her hands in her pockets.

"So, Australia, huh?"

"I know, right? What an opportunity." Around me, my eyes wander to the people who surround us. "I'm gonna miss this crazy group of ours."

"And we'll miss you, too." She grins, knocking my arm with hers.

For most of the afternoon, we have fun eating and being merry. Hazel doesn't hold back in cooking up a storm despite my attempt to help her in the kitchen which she flat out refused.

Jerry immerses himself in playing with Andy. I have never seen him like this—alive, full of smiles. I can't help but notice how happy it makes Hazel to see him like this, given his previous hatred for children. Andy is lapping up the attention, and Jerry, he's like a little boy again, chasing the dogs and playing fetch.

Fred is busy teaching Tristan how to play Mahjong. Tristan is a gamer, so he can't be any more in his element. Fred enjoys sharing his wisdom and knowledge with others as it gives him a sense of worth, building the strength he needs to overcome his fears and live a normal life.

Eric and Penny are immersed in a hair conversation. I choose to zone out, there's only so much conversation involving hair I can deal with. You might think by looking at their body language that it's a heated debate on Russian politics, when all along it's simply about bangs.

Adriana and Hazel bring out a cake—chocolate and covered in sprinkles. It looks delicious. Jerry and Andy run toward them, almost knocking them over.

"I love chocolate sprinkles," Jerry says excitedly.

"Me, too, Jerry! We can be best friends now... pretty please?" Andy begs.

"Sure, why not, kid?" Jerry gives him a genuine smile.

Hazel slices the cake and hands everyone a piece. I guess it's time for me to make a speech, something I want to do to express my gratitude.

I quickly ask for everyone's attention, the voices softening until there's only the sound of a warm breeze rustling the trees.

"This is, well... surreal," I begin, clearing my throat to sort through my overpowering emotions. "I came to this group searching for help, support, something to get me through this thing we call life. I found that, but most importantly, I found a family."

Hazel is by my side dabbing her eyes, a rare side to her since she always seems in control of her emotions. Yet standing beside me, I sense her pride.

"I never thought I was worthy of anything, let alone anyone, but every person in this room has welcomed me into their life despite my flaws and mistakes. It has helped me make the right decisions, and for that, I'll be forever grateful."

Penny raises her can of soda before clutching it to her chest with pride much like Hazel.

"If I can say a few words." She clears her throat, taking center stage. "Julian, you're an unbelievably gorgeous man, and I mean spanking-take-you-to-bed-in-a-heartbeat gorgeous!"

We all laugh. Thankfully, Andy has already walked away.

"That's on the outside. On the inside, you have a heart of gold. The first man not to be ashamed of who I am despite my inappropriate advances. You saw me for who I am... Peter... a lonely boy who wants to be loved, who wants to be just like everyone else and not hide the real me. You welcomed me into your life, and I'm going to miss your companionship. Who's gonna take me to bingo night?"

"Bingo? Oh, I love it," Eric squeals. "It's so *Golden Girls*... I'm so in!"

I shake my head, grinning as Eric basks in his newfound hobby—replacing me at bingo night.

Fred and Jerry say a few words, followed by Hazel. It's without fail, Hazel's kind words give me the confidence I need to leave this place, but only temporarily.

"This place here, Julian, is always your home," she adds, with a smile. "It's a home for all of you. Welcoming you at your time of need, your time of peace, and holds no judgment because you are all worthy of being here."

Penny lets out a loud wail, forcing us to all turn her way. Fred, being a father himself, places his hand on Penny's shoulder and hands her his handkerchief. Taking it, Penny blows her nose loudly, then hands it back, much to Fred's discomfort.

Adriana clears her throat, wanting to speak. "I need to get Andy home. It's past his bedtime."

Slightly offended, I offer to round up Ash and help take him to her car, ignoring this unwarranted hurt festering inside of me. This isn't a moment to allow my selfish need to justify my actions. Adriana needs space, time, and despite my yearning to build something between us greater than a friendship, our paths are not in sync.

She buckles Andy in who is exhausted from all the running around. Shutting the door behind her, she turns to face me. "Thank you for being a friend," she whispers, unable to look me in the eye.

"Wouldn't have it any other way. Take care of yourself, Adriana."

She nods and moves toward the car. I want so much to embrace her, hold her in my arms since I don't know when I'll see her next, but she needs her time, and I can't push her.

"Bye, Julian. Take care of yourself as well, okay?"

Slowly, her eyes move upward until our gaze locks. Finally, I see inside her soul, understand her pain, her conflict, the battle between her head and heart. The unspoken words between us are greater than any words said out loud. I know this time it's not my imagination. I've learned from my mistakes and forcing her to feel the same way about me isn't an option.

Adriana is like a wilted flower, and with the correct love and attention, she'll blossom again. I may not be that person for her, but one thing I know for sure there is no one else who deserves to find happiness as much as Adriana. She's a warrior. She experienced love and loss, wearing her battle scars as a reminder that her love can't be forgotten. Anyone who comes close to that will never replace him.

But a close second is all I can hope for.

EPILOGUE

The fast bustle of the travelers disguises me as I sit on the row of seats, ticket in one hand and a heavy heart in the other.

Even in the presence of so many people, my loneliness is palpable. Once again, I'm on a journey with myself, willing to discover what makes my heart beat with joy.

This is the right thing to do.

Moving to Australia for six months will be a once-in-a-lifetime opportunity, and one I can't miss because of mixed emotions. My heart is sobbing like a lovesick fool, but it's my head waving its flag saying, *"Listen to me for once."*

And so, I do.

Adriana deserves better. She deserves a man who'll love her and Andy unconditionally, together as a whole. And most importantly, she deserves it at the right time, not pushed upon her during her time of grief.

Do I love her?

I feel something, but I'm in denial. You see, Julian Baker has a habit of falling head over heels in love but always to forget.

Adriana doesn't replace anyone.

She stands on her own.

And I need to walk away to make sure my feelings are justified. Yet, unlike every other time I walked away, usually from a bruised ego, this moment is different.

I feel sick to my stomach. The pain, indescribable, serves a purpose. We're both forced to rediscover who we are in this game called life. I'm yet to understand why we're forced through this insurmountable pain to find the so-called rainbow.

The announcement is made for the final boarding call thousands of miles across the ocean. I honestly can't be going further away from her. I grab my carry-on and join the line. Slowly, like a marching order, we walk, filing into one line.

There's a family in front of me—father, mother, and two young children. The children are running around the parents much to their frustration. Inside the arms of the mother, she's carrying what appears to be a newborn child. Even amid the chaos, she rocks the baby with a content smile.

I'm not oblivious to the scene before me, understanding there's a greater, more unconditional love than between a man and woman. It's one of a mother and child, a bond so secure nothing in this world can ever break it. With that thought, I make a mental note to call my mom the moment I land just to let her know I have arrived safely.

Suddenly, my focus shifts as I hear my name being called. With the noise of the people around me, plus the speakers making several announcements, I assume it's my imagination.

Just move on.

My name is called again, it's getting closer, and as I turn

around I see Adriana running toward me, pushing others out of the way until she's in front of me. She places her hands on her knees, trying to catch her breath.

I pull her aside, worried she's about to collapse on the spot from a heart attack. Despite her thin frame, she isn't lying when she claims she's unfit.

"Adriana? What are you doing here?"

She attempts to talk but is halted by the lack of air in her lungs. "Oh my God, I'm so unfit."

I let out a laugh. Putting my bag down, I gently say her name again. With her big green eyes, she stares back at me, desperately trying to talk with her eyes rather than her mouth.

"I don't know what will happen. I can't make promises. There's only one thing I'm sure of... I want to live to see Andy grow. And..." she watches me as she speaks, her eyes wide, a mixture of fear and desperation, "... I want to see where we can go. It'll be hard, I know. My brother, he'll kill me, but this is my life, and I can't deny my feelings anymore."

My heavy chest lightens as she says the words I so desperately want to hear, yet never realized how much until this very moment.

I wipe the tear falling on her face, brushing my thumb against her lip willing the tears to stop.

Everything she wants, everything my heart so desperately needs, is standing right in front of us. Except for one thing—a plane outside this terminal ready to take me away on my next journey. My lips press together in a slight grimace, conflicted as to what to do.

But what's the rush?

We have forever, right?

"I have to do this, Adriana. I have to go find myself, but..." I search her face, praying she understands the importance of me leaving, "... I want to see where this can go, too."

She stands in front of me, shuffling her feet with a huge grin on her face. Her body relaxes, but I know not to take this too far. As Hazel said, she's living and breathing. There are ways to make this work. I don't need to rush fate or whatever the hell it is that brings us into each other's lives.

"Promise you'll email?" she asks.

"I promise to email."

Adriana purses her lips. "Promise you'll call?"

"I promise to call."

The announcement blares over the speakers, and the line is becoming shorter. With only minutes left, I think carefully about the right move to make.

"I don't expect you to wait for me, Julian. In fact, if you find someone, you know... like to—"

I cut her off and place my hand into hers. "Adriana... you're worth waiting for."

And with that, I raise her hand toward my mouth and tilt it sideways, placing my lips on the scars covering her wrists. Kissing them sends a warm rush within me, and in this moment, I know why everything that happened before this moment did happen.

All in this one kiss.

I know I want nothing more than to show her how strong my feelings are, and the best thing I can do for us right now is to heal on my own.

"Thank you," she mouths, the beautiful smile on her face rocking me to the core.

I let go, not forever, but for right now and walk away knowing good things come to those who wait.

And Adriana Evans is a *great* thing.

To be continued...

CHASING HIM

Chasing Him
A Forbidden Second Chance Romance
The Dark Love Series Book 4

BLURB

Our vows were exchanged.
We had our whole lives planned out.
And even brought our son into this world.
Until hours later... when everything stopped, and you were
suddenly gone.

Life was perfect until the day the only man she had ever
been with, the man who had stolen her heart at the tender
age of seventeen, was taken away before his time.

Desperate, angry, and unable to heal, Adriana hits rock
bottom and is forced to seek help for the sake of her son.
What she doesn't expect is a friendship from an unlikely
source—Julian Baker, her best friend's ex-fiancé.

Julian is every bit the man she isn't expecting to walk into her life—intelligent, witty, and extremely handsome. Their unique friendship soon turns into a forbidden relationship. As lovers, they form a bond that must remain hidden from their family and friends, but secrets can only be kept for so long.

Adriana's brother, Lex, loathes Julian and will stop at nothing to break them apart.

Will Lex's controlling nature and overprotective stance on his wife drive Adriana to end another great love in her life? Or will she finally heal with a man who never intended to steal her heart?

ALSO BY KAT T. MASEN

The Dark Love Series

Featuring Lex & Charlie

Chasing Love: A Billionaire Love Triangle

Chasing Us: A Second Chance Love Triangle

Chasing Her: A Stalker Romance

Chasing Him: A Forbidden Second Chance Romance

Chasing Fate: An Enemies-to-Lovers Romance

Chasing Heartbreak: A Friends-to-Lovers Romance

The Forbidden Love Series

(Dark Love Series Second Generation)

Featuring Amelia Edwards

The Trouble With Love: An Age Gap Romance

The Trouble With Us: A Second Chance Love Triangle

The Trouble With Him: A Secret Pregnancy Romance

The Trouble With Her: A Friends-to-Lovers Romance

The Trouble With Fate: An Enemies-to-Lovers Romance

The Office Rival: An Enemies-to-Lovers Romance

The Marriage Rival: An Office Romance

Bad Boy Player: A Brother's Best Friend Romance

Roomie Wars Box Set (Books 1 to 3): Friends-to-Lovers Series

ABOUT THE AUTHOR

Born and bred in Sydney, Australia, **Kat T. Masen** is a mother to four crazy boys and wife to one sane husband. Growing up in a generation where social media and fancy gadgets didn't exist, she enjoyed reading from an early age and found herself immersed in these stories. After meeting friends on Twitter who loved to read as much as she did, her passion for writing began, and the friendships continued on despite the distance.

"I'm known to be crazy and humorous. Show me the most random picture of a dog in a wig, and I'll be laughing for days."

Download free bonus content, purchase signed paperbacks & bookish merchandise.

Visit: **www.kattmasen.com**

Made in the USA
Middletown, DE
14 October 2023